Annual Survey of
American Poetry: 1985

Poetry Anthology Press

The World's Best Poetry

Survey of American Poetry

Annual Survey of American Poetry: 1985

Prepared by

The Editorial Board, Roth Publishing, Inc.
(formerly Granger Book Co., Inc.)

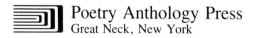 Poetry Anthology Press
Great Neck, New York

Copyright © 1987 Roth Publishing, Inc.
All rights reserved

The acknowledgments on pages 291–298
constitute a continuation of this copyright
notice.

Library of Congress Catalog Number 86-62135
International Standard Book Number 0-89609-266-6
International Standard Serial Number 0889-4450

Manufactured in the U.S.A.

Poetry Anthology Press is a
division of Roth Publishing, Inc.
(formerly Granger Book Co., Inc.)

CONTENTS

PREFACE

The publications of **Poetry Anthology Press** constitute a comprehensive conspectus of international verse in English designed to form the core of a library's poetry collection. Covering the entire range of poetic literature, these anthologies encompass all topics and national literatures.

Each collection, published in a multivolume continuing series format, is devoted to a major area of the whole undertaking and contains complete author, title, and first line indexes. Biographical data is also provided.

The World's Best Poetry, with coverage through the 19th century, is topically classified and arranged by subject matter. Supplements keep the 10 volume foundation collection current and complete.

Survey of American Poetry is an anthology of American verse arranged chronologically in 10 volumes. Each volume presents a significant period of American poetic history, from 1607 to 1984. *Annual Survey of American Poetry* continues the coverage and maintains the currency of the collection.

INTRODUCTION

In the tradition of the ten-volume *Survey of American Poetry, Annual Survey of American Poetry* continues to chronicle the nation's poetic development. While the foundation set covers American verse from 1607–1984, the *Annual Survey* series offers a year by year sampling of new American poetry beginning with this 1985 edition. *Annual Survey of American Poetry: 1985* contains an array of over one hundred never before anthologized poems by a variety of poets, recognized as well as up-and-coming. The poetry chosen for this volume represents current incarnations of past trends, as well as new developments. However, despite the literary diversity, most of these works may be categorized according to several prevalent genres.

One such genre is the conversational poem. Designed to be entertaining, the conversational poem is written in a casual, anecdotal style and depends more on the poet's charisma than on the events that are being recounted. In fact, as the subject matter becomes more prosaic, the poet's charm is shown to greater advantage. The art of enchanting artlessly is aptly demonstrated in "The Sickness" by Charles Bukowski, who has been writing in this style for over twenty years. However, Bukowski's raw and energetic quality is a rarity among the sophisticated and witty tone that has recently come to dominate poetry of this type. Tom Disch, Howard Nemerov, Raymond Carver, Lydia Davis, and Patricia Storace are just a few of the writers publishing today who have adopted this highly amusing style.

In poetry that focuses on introspective inquiry rather than on showmanship, theories of human psychology have been enormously influential. Confessional poetry, for example, has borrowed many themes from Freudian psychology, while deep imagism, new surrealism, and mystic poetry contain ideas common to Jungian psychology. These forms are still in practice today, although each has been modified from its midcentury inception. (For a look at the various poetic styles of the last three decades, see the Introduction to volume ten of *Survey of American Poetry: Midcentury to 1984*.)

The confessional school's morbid beginnings have become quite infamous. Though less sensational than it was thirty years ago, contemporary confessional poetry is still intensely stirring. The portrayal of the individual's private side, with all its latent psychological tensions, is now depicted within the context of a normal, healthy mind. "In the Hospital, Near the End" by Sharon Olds and "I'm Not Complaining" by Philip Schultz exemplify this new trend. If there remains any lingering fascination with the madness which was inherent to this form, it is the madness of a sensitive, thoughtful individual surviving in a chaotic, violent, and sometimes marvelous world. Confessional poetry's emotional response to the world, no longer limited to extreme psychological states, invites greater empathy from its audience than did the shocking poems that introduced the genre.

Deep imagism, another midcentury innovation, was initially designed to express deep subconscious meanings through a system of cryptic symbols. More common today, however, is the use of one central symbol to resonate meaning throughout the poem. Horses and snakes, for example, have both been associated with human sexuality throughout literary history. By employing these symbols, Lucinda Grealy in "Ferrying Horses" and Wendell Berry in "The Snake" convert ordinary events into highly charged emotional realities.

New surrealism was first practiced during the late sixties. Infused with a playful spirit, this poetry is unrestrained, illogical, and often very funny. Though it appears to be impulsively and thoughtlessly written, there is an operative methodology at work. This type of poem attempts to subvert logical expectations and old language habits so that provocative, new associations may arise. Its initial shock value has worn off somewhat over the last fifteen years, yet when the ludicrous is mixed with the usual, as is the current use of this form, new surrealism becomes an ironic comment on our everyday speech and rutted perceptions. "The Road Between Here and There" by Galway Kinnell and "Happy End" by Charles Simic demonstrate this style.

Mystic poetry has largely become a West Coast phenomenon, as only a few poets there continue to write in this style. It is a genre steeped in allusions to ancient religious texts, esoteric anthropological sources, and the occult sciences. The typical themes of mystic poetry are revelations of primordial secrets, a clear understanding of present times, and prophecies of the future; a combination of specialized knowledge and inspiration is what informs this poetry. However, mystic poetry today has acquired a darker tone than it had during the sixties when it first became popular. Instead of the air of hope encouraged by the idealism of the sixties, the present trend toward materialism and the shadow of nuclear destruction may be what is coloring this form with a sense of alienation and apocalypse, as is evident in Nathaniel Mackey's poem, "The Phantom Light of All Our Day."

Another genre that became popular during the late sixties is socio-political poetry. Though anti-war and anti-discrimination protest poems were the mainstay of the form's turbulent beginnings, poets today continue to write about topical concerns, including feminism, poverty, ethnicity, the anti-nuclear movement, and current world events. Poems such as Philip Levine's "Sweet Will" and Brenda Marie Osbey's "The Factory Poem" demonstrate a socially aware brand of poetics.

Not all poetic forms practiced today are midcentury innovations. Lyric poetry, narrative poetry, and dramatic poetry have been the vehicles for poetic inspiration since ancient times. These forms have survived over the years by accommodating a wide variety of writing styles. The introspective musings of the lyric, for example, are demonstrated this year by the diverse talents of Denise Levertov, Faye Kicknosway, and Hilda Morley.

The dramatic poem is responsible for some of the best loved literary characters of all time. More demanding and more formal than the lyric, the dramatic tradition is continued this year by such skilled writers as Howard Moss and Mary Tisera. Grace Paley lends to this form a humorous twist by creating a non-human character, and David Denny's impression of Holden Caulfield, the main character of *Catcher in the Rye*, also puts this form to comic use.

The narrative poem has regained popularity after being out of fashion for some time. During 1985 the form has thrived. Jane Kenyon, Garrett Kaoru Hongo, David Ray, Henry Taylor, and Michael Waters, to name a few, contribute their unique phraseologies and memories to this form. Robert McDowell's "Quiet Money" exemplifies the style of the longer narrative poem which is almost indistinguishable from a short story. Marilyn Hacker adds another dimension by relating her story in verse.

The return of structured forms in verse is also characteristic of the mid eighties. After years of poetry written predominantly in free verse, 1985 marks the publication of sonnets by John Updike and Mary Jo Salter, a pantoum by Marc Cohen, the rhymed iambic pentameter of X.J. Kennedy and Allen Hoey, as well as the irregular rhymes of Robert Penn Warren.

Nevertheless, the poetry of the eighties is not entirely comprised of prefabricated forms. Language poems are the artistic manifestations of current literary theory. Deconstructionism, the name given to the latest critical method, asserts that a piece of literature contains not one meaning but multiple possibilities for meaning. Philosophically akin to this theory, language poetry is composed of disparate elements which are linked through associations of sound and thought. These poems do not offer predetermined conclusions; instead, thought is displayed as an open-ended process. Often this is done in a playful manner: "IV./Ivy that is./Had you forgotten" (Pamela Alexander's "Vines"). Roots of this current academic movement and its corresponding poetic expression are traceable to contemporary French philosophy and turn-of-the-century Russian poetry. In America, the avant-garde poetry of the New York School preceded this trend by many years. The poem "Oleum Misericordiae," first published in the now classic *Self-Portrait in a Convex Mirror*, is a timely reminder of John Ashbery's influential role in this latest development of contemporary American poetry.

The proliferation of poetry in America today is evinced by the yearly outpouring of books and periodicals and by the many writing programs and awards devoted to poetry. It thrives in spite of remaining outside mainstream popular culture. The underground artistic energy extends to urban center and countryside, to academician and businessman, to professional writer and avocational writer; in short, contemporary American poets defy all stereotypes. The diverse body of work they produce results in the democracy of methods, ideas, literary histories, and cultural roots that compose the state of the literary art.

Pamela Alexander

Born in Natick, Massachusetts in 1948, Pamela Alexander received a B.A. from Bates College and an M.F.A. from the University of Iowa. Her first book, *Navigable Waterways* (Yale: 1985), won the 1984 Yale Series of Younger Poets competition. Alexander contributes frequently to literary magazines, and her work can be found in *The Atlantic Monthly*, *Anima*, *The Antioch Review*, *Field*, *Poetry*, and *Poetry Now*.

Vines

A.
Acacia. flowering and an archway.
A round ambush = an abyssinian cat.
Consider lines as small events:
a curled cat uncurling.
Consider events as places to live, and
　　　　paragraphing
　　　　　　　as paper sculpture.

A polygon has many angels.
How many cousins to the ounce?
How many weasels to the once?
Consider the shapes breath makes: words　　　clouds
coins in the blood
florins.

A flourish.

II.
Two parts. Often it does.
mountain and river.
First loss lasts
and fills itself
with glosses.

B. the glass blower.
His breath closes open air, makes
spaces into shapes.
Bottles   clear or amber
a green glass
a blue dress:
he says can I look at them all
all at once.
          Eyes
small rooms to hold worlds   cities, woods
and the wide shadows of words travelling toward the sun.
She says may I look at you.

IV.
Ivy that is.
Had you forgotten.
X.

Winter a white angle.
A gable.
Gabriel at the table, upon it
is oil.   precious.   pressure.
In a brown bottle a crush of prehistoric fern.

V.
The leaves he showed her became the first she'd seen.
She is a shape in space containing many things;
where his eyes burned her there is

room for tigers
        the Tigris

        irises
        one ibis

        two.

John Ashbery

John Ashbery was born in 1927, in Rochester, New York. He received a B.A. in literature from Harvard University and an M.A. from Columbia University. In 1955 he was awarded a Fulbright Scholarship to study in France, where he lived for a decade. While in France, Ashbery wrote art criticism for the European edition of the *New York Herald Tribune* and served as a foreign correspondent for *Art News*. In 1956 Ashbery's book, *Some Trees*, was selected for the Yale Younger Poets Series. Since then his poetry has won numerous awards, including the National Book Award, the National Book Critics Award, and the Pulitzer Prize for *Self-Portrait in a Convex Mirror* (1975).

Oleum Misericordiae

To rub it out, make it less virulent
And a stab too at rearranging
The whole thing from the ground up.
Yes we were waiting just now
Yes we are no longer waiting.

Afterwards when I tell you
It's as though it all only happened
As siding of my story

I beg you to listen
You are already listening

4

It has shut itself out
And in doing so shut us accidentally in

And meanwhile my story goes well
The first chapter
    endeth

But the real story, the one
They tell us we shall probably never know
Drifts back in bits and pieces
All of them, it turns out

So lucky
Now we really know
It all happened by chance:
A chance encounter
The dwarf led you to the end of a street
And pointed flapping his arms in two directions
You forgot to misprize him
But after a series of interludes
In furnished rooms (describe wallpaper)
Transient hotels (mention sink and cockroaches)
And spending the night with a beautiful married woman
Whose husband was away in Centerville on business
(Mention this wallpaper: the purest roses
Though the creamiest and how
Her smile lightens the ordeal
Of the last 500 pages
Though you never knew her last name
Only her first: Dorothy)
You got hold of the water of life
Rescued your two wicked brothers Cash and Jethro
Who promptly stole the water of life
After which you got it back, got safely home.
Saved the old man's life
And inherited the kingdom.

But this was a moment
Under the most cheerful sun.
In poorer lands
No one touches the water of life.

It has no taste
And though it refreshes absolutely
It is a cup that must also pass

Until everybody
Gets some advantage, big or little
Some reason for having come
So far
Without dog or woman
So far alone, unasked.

Susan Astor

Susan Astor's first book, *Dame*, was published in 1980 as part of the Contemporary Poetry Series of the University of Georgia Press. Her awards include the *Carolina Quarterly* Poetry Prize and the Triton International Poetry Prize. Astor's poems have appeared in *West Hills Review*, *The Paris Review*, *Shenandoah*, *Kansas Quarterly*, *Confrontation*, and *Partisan Review*. She currently resides in Roslyn Heights, New York.

Mother's Day

Stroking you, I think of her
how much she loved you then, her little boy,
how much she did not mean to die.
I run my fingertip around your ear
and think how pleased you must have been
          to hear her voice.
Did she hide kisses on your neck
          the way I do?
Like me, she knew you in the dark
your secret smells
the sounds you breathe in sleep.
I vow to keep whatever promises she made
    when she first let you out into the world
          so small, so unprepared.
Now that you're big and strong
    I take you in.

Jane Augustine

Born in Berkeley, California in 1931, Jane Augustine was educated
at Bryn Mawr College and at Washington University. A writer of
poetry, fiction, and criticism, she has received fellowships in poetry
from the New York State Council on the Arts in 1976 and 1979. Her
collection, *Lit by the Earth's Dark Blood*, was published in 1977; her
short story, "Secretive," appears in *Images of Women in Literature*.
Augustine is currently a Ph.D. candidate at the City University of
New York and is teaching at Pratt Institute in Brooklyn and at The
New School, in New York City.

For Meg
(on her 24th birthday)

October dusk: we're walking east on 60th street.

As many years of my life have passed
since your birth as before it—
from now on I am clearly more mother than child.

Dry leaves blow from planetrees onto stoops
of brownstones. You, my autumn daughter, in russet
blouse and fawn-beige skirt, stride beside me

firmly, as if I were in your charge, might go
astray. Apparently I've given you my strengths
and certainties, left myself with questions,

ruminations which seem to you too fragile,
remnants of oak and maple. Leaves swirl around us,
making the fall wind's power visible. Secretly

I still want to teach you, not how to master the world
any more, but how to trust it, let its beauty happen.
    Tomorrow you fly back to Paris. Now we stand

on this broken leafstrewn curb, a balance-point,
your birthday, when I came to life as your mother,
and you, strong as now in your first push outward,

took on the burden of my courage which lets you go.

Tina Barr

Born in New York City in 1955, Tina Barr received a B.A. from
Sarah Lawrence College and an M.F.A. from Columbia University.
Her chapbook, *At Dusk on Naskeag Point*, won the Flume Press
Annual Poetry Chapbook Contest in 1984, and during the same year
she was awarded a fellowship in literature from the Pennsylvania
Council on the Arts. Barr has taught at Villanova University and at
Temple University, where she is currently an M.A. candidate.

Public Garden Above the Rhone

In the public garden
that hangs in the air
above the Pont d'Avignon
behind the Palais des Papes,
where seven popes ruled from their fortress,
you hold my arm, while the wind,
the mistral, lifts the purse from my side,
my skirt above my thighs.
But here, no one looks
and if I hold your arm
two women, who touch,
no one turns their head to stare.

The german girl's skirt
rises and luffs in the wind
and a young man, bending his knees,

takes a picture
as she presses her skirt down.
The mountains, where Cezanne painted
the thrust of the earth's shoulder
creep up over her shoulder.

But what he cannot take
is a picture of the wind
as it shows itself
running like current
on the terraced lawn below,
as it lifts each sliver of grass,
makes troughs and gulleys.
And he cannot capture the comet trails
of its path, visible in the grass,
waves of heat sheening.

The wind shows us this,
some message, some image,
in the lawns of public gardens
in this country, where wisteria
grows in a museum courtyard
and I can gather
the weight of its blossoms
to my chest and inhale its scent.
In this country the lady
who runs the hotel smiles
and pleats the edge of a napkin at her table.

Wendell Berry

Wendell Berry was born in Henry County, Kentucky, in 1934. He received a B.A. and an M.A. from the University of Kentucky, where he taught English from 1964 until 1977. Berry is an essayist, a novelist, and the author of over one dozen books of poetry. His honors include fellowships from the Guggenheim and Rockefeller Foundations and a National Endowment for the Arts Grant.

The Snake

At the end of October
I found on the floor of the woods
a small snake whose back
was patterned with the dark
of the dead leaves he lay on.
His body was thickened with a mouse
or small bird. He was cold,
so stuporous with his full belly
and the fall air that he hardly
troubled to flicker his tongue.
I held him a long time, thinking
of the perfection of the dark
marking on his back, the death
that swelled him, his living cold.
Now the cold of him stays

in my hand, and I think of him
lying below the frost,
big with a death to nourish him
during a long sleep.

Robert Bly

Born in Madison, Minnesota in 1926, Robert Bly received an A.B. from Harvard University in 1950 and an M.A. from the University of Iowa in 1956. During World War II, he served in the United States Navy. He has written over twenty books of original poetry and is a well-known translator of literature; he has made over twenty-five books accessible to English speaking audiences. Bly was editor of the decade-spanning magazine and press *The Fifties* (later *The Sixties* and *The Seventies*) and, with David Ray, edited the anthology *A Poetry Reading Against the Vietnam War* (1966). He has received the Amy Lowell Travelling Fellowship, a National Book Award, and a Guggenheim Fellowship, and he currently gives readings at colleges and universities across the country.

A Third Body

A man and a woman sit near each other, and they do
     not long
at this moment to be older, or younger, nor born
in any other nation, or time, or place.
They are content to be where they are, talking or
     not-talking.
Their breaths together feed someone whom we do
     not know.
The man sees the way his fingers move;
he sees her hands close around a book she hands
     to him.

14

They obey a third body that they share in common.
They have made a promise to love that body.
Age may come, parting may come, death will come.
A man and a woman sit near each other;
as they breathe they feed someone we do not know,
someone we know of, whom we have never seen.

Donald Britton

Born in Texas in 1951, Donald Britton received a B.A. and an M.A. from the University of Texas and a Ph.D. from The American University. *Italy*, a collection of his poetry, was published by Little Caesar Press in 1981. His poems have appeared in numerous publications, including *The Paris Review*, *Oink!*, *Epoch*, and *Poetry in Motion*. Britton is a copywriter for a Manhattan marketing group. He lives in New York City.

In the Empire of the Air

Scourging the sea with rods
To punish it for what it has engulfed,
Or running naked with your bronzed friend
Through yellow broomsage:
You can't be sure which remedy will be
Fatal, or whether the density of the side effects
Will prevent you from moving backwards
Across the threshold, to read
What the instructions might have said
If anyone had taken time to write them down,
So we could torture the words, make them
Confess their dirty little secret. It's tiered,
As earth is, with faults perfectly expressing
A gravitational will that we should stumble
Over them. And all the hints
Get sponged up at night. Above the land fill—

Stars, glowing zircon strands of dump truck highbeams
Lined up, liquid and radiant, past the last
Open-all-night erotica boutique
Just over the state line of the last state.
Maybe they're sparks we ignite
Rubbing each other the wrong way, fiery notes
Unwary rhapsodists pluck from the strings
Of incendiary violins. Is that what you think, too?
In truth, I prefer your mistaken identity,
The upside down one I can see at the back of my eyes
Before they flip you into focus, projecting you
Across a space at once so vast and so small
As not to excite even scientific curiosity.
But the light you throw off, out there,
Is not enough to see you by. The tapered crimps
And ridges, scraped into the wall of the well,
Could be any number of people. Try
To communicate with the dying sometime
And you'll know what I mean. Each one is perfect,
Of its kind. Also, all are alike. Not even they
Can tell you, though, where the similarities end,
Whether it will be any different
For you. All I know is that what you are
To the waxed, limpid air of freak May in December
Or to this room, piled high
With genial household archetypes,
Is a formal relation only, as the shape
Of an airplane-shaped shrub is
To the living plant it's made of. But to me,
And all I said and did, and all the time
It took me to get here, so much I forgot
The purpose of my visit, but kept on anyway; to me,
As I hold you, and the messy edges
Of our privacy overlap and then withdraw—
Think of me as three persons, and as one,
But always who I am, ever changing

And complete, in the empire of the air
Or on the street, or with white sails
Stiff against the wind,
Whistling far out over the water.

Charles Bukowski

Born in Andernach, Germany in 1920, Charles Bukowski immigrated to the United States at the age of three and was raised in Los Angeles. He attended Los Angeles City College from 1939 until 1941. Though his first story was published when he was twenty-four, he did not write poetry until he was thirty-five. Beginning with his first book, *Flower, Fist and Bestial Wail* (1960), his books number over forty to date, and his poetry and fiction have been translated into dozens of languages. *War All the Time* (1984) is his latest book.

the sickness

if
one night
I write
what I consider to
be
5 or 6 good poems
then I begin
to worry:

suppose the house
burns down?

I'm not worried
about
the house

I'm worried
about
those 5 or 6
poems
burning
up

or

an x-girlfriend
getting in
here
while I'm away
and stealing or
destroying
the poems.

after writing
5 or 6 poems
I am fairly
drunk
and
I sit
having a few
more
drinks
while deciding
where to hide
the poems.

sometimes I
hide the poems
while
thinking about
hiding
them

and when I
decide to
hide them
I can't find
them . . .

then
begins the
search

and the
whole room is
a mass of
papers
anyhow

and

I'm very clever
at
hiding poems
perhaps more
clever than I
am
at
writing
them.

so
then
I find them
have another
drink

hide them
again

forget it
then
go
to sleep . . .

to awaken in
late morning
to remember
the poems
and
begin the
search
again . . .

usually only a
ten or fifteen
minute
period of
agony

to find
them
and read
them
and then
not like them
very much

but you know
after all
that
work

all that
drinking
hiding

searching
finding

I decide
it's only
fair
to send
them
out
as a
record of
my travail

which
if accepted
will appear in
a little
magazine
circulation
between
100 and
750

a year-and
one-half
later

maybe.

it's
worth
it.

Barney Bush

Born in 1946, Barney Bush is a Native American poet of Shawnee and Cayuga descent. He was educated at Fort Lewis College and at the University of Idaho. *Inherit the Blood*, his fourth book, was published in 1986. Bush has travelled throughout North America, giving readings and leading workshops. His honors include a National Endowment for the Arts Award. He currently lives with his son in northern Vermont.

Silent Witness
for Bud
Spring '84

It was last nights moon
that brought   the
sound   voices in the
creek   erupting in
nights reflections
dissolving in spring
runoff   as that
ancestral moon of ours
that round glowing face
that has viewed all of
nighttimes history
stared into my own   She
is our grandmother   but
i cry out to one who sees

24

through day and night
and to you who begins the
last distance of the sacred
journey   you who has
left this awesome distance
these memories of when we
were first walking upright
hurling razor edged knives
to the boundaries of human
flesh   spread eagled to
the barn   and plotted
sinister hoaxes at community
rituals   Even in
sunlit forest journeys
swimming holes   there were
desperate retreats on horses
backs   and
that first time below humid
ancients grounds   at
the creekbank door   within
the circle of sunlight
where birds grew silent on
limbs   salty beads
erupted from brown pores
stinging the eyes   the
lips
It was a ceremony   ours
as we shared the blood
Below the hill of ancient ones
whose silence was broken by
the pounding of our hearts
we could smell the damp
broken soil   a spring wind
that almost wailed   almost
mourned for us   Sometimes
i still wake whispering your
name.

Hayden Carruth

Born in New England in 1921, Hayden Carruth studied at the University of North Carolina and at the University of Chicago. He served with the Army Air Corps during World War II. An editor of *Poetry* magazine in the late forties, Carruth was also the poetry editor of *Harper's* magazine and an advisory editor for *The Hudson Review*. He has published sixteen books of poetry, the most recent being *If You Call This Cry a Song*. His poems have also appeared in hundreds of magazines. Although Carruth was a long-time Vermont resident, he has been teaching at Syracuse University for the past few years.

Plain Song

After the storm a peculiar
    calm crept over us, a
hush. Everything was white, the roads
    were vanished. Superla-

tives upon superlatives of
    snow transcended any-
thing anyone could say. The roof
    of T.J.'s Family

Restaurant that had lifted and
    turned and sailed a hundred

feet onto my patio, in-
to my glass doors, was bed-

ded against my sofa now un-
der a blanket of snow.
It's no rarity here; we have
big storms that come and go

all winter, and some are true bliz-
zards. But hell, this one ex-
ceeded all records, all measure-
ments. It was huge, complex,

unbelievable. It was Su-
perbliz. Then it was si-
lence, at least at first, a force as
awesome and broad and high

as the roaring and wreckage of
the storm itself, nature's
two utterly opposite as-
pects, between which adverse-

ly we human creatures shrank to
nothing. No voice, no mach-
ine. Only the snow. Where we had
become used to the trash

of the strip, all the gaudy plas-
tic of the fast food chains
and filling stations, the dete-
rioration, dirt, stains

of rust and corruption, brok-
en glass, now the snow spread
smooth and swirling over every-
thing: from our upper bed-

room windows we saw it. Silence
and snow. Sleekly soft, fan-
ciful as dunes. "Who killed Cock Rob-
in?" "Who knows?" "Who cares?" Can-

cer is the answer, like every-
body. And the snow got
holes in it very quickly, the
bridal gown was forgot-

ten, lying motheaten, and so
was the bride, her bones show-
ing through. The children gave up their
prayers and began to crow

in welcome of noise again, the
great machine making fount-
ains of dirty, slushy, slimy
snow. Somewhere the account-

ants got busy with new figures.
"Even steven, all is
less." So it took three days to get
all the cars dug out, this

being what mattered, of course. For
those three days people laughed
and joked, spoke of the Donner Pass
and Admiral Byrd. Aft-

er that the old anxiety
and greed settled back on,
grimace and pain. The TV came
back. We were not aston-

ished to find it was Christmas. The
    kids danced to see the lights
of the shrieking ambulances
    again, filling the nights

with comfortable nips of hor-
    ror. I paid, myself, to
have the patio and doors re-
    paired. Who wants to go through

all the red tape for a disas-
    ter loan? There's where they spliced
the railing, hardly noticea-
    ble now under the Christ-

ly multiplications of clem-
    atis, though that's what turned
my thoughts back now on this hot night
    to Superbliz. Who learned

anything from it? Ten feet of
    snow in 24 hours,
December 1983—
    the biggest, and all ours.

But nobody remembers. All
    days are records. I won-
der what it would really take to
    grab people's attention?

Raymond Carver

Born in 1939, Raymond Carver is a poet and fiction writer. He has taught at the University of Iowa, the University of Texas, the University of California, and at Syracuse University, where he resigned his chair in 1983 to accept a Mildred and Harold Living Award. His story, "A Small, Good Thing," won first place in William Abraham's distinguished short fiction annual, *Prize Stories: The O. Henry Awards*. In addition to his works of fiction, Carver has written three volumes of poetry. A recipient of two National Endowment for the Arts Grants and a Guggenheim Fellowship, Carver's most recent book of poetry is *Where Water Comes Together with Other Water* (Random House: 1985). He currently resides in the Pacific Northwest.

Locking Yourself Out, Then Trying To Get Back In

You simply go out and shut the door
without thinking. And when you look back
at what you've done
it's too late. If this sounds
like the story of a life, okay.

It was raining. The neighbors who had
a key were away. I tried and tried
the lower windows. Stared
inside at the sofa, plants, the table
and chairs, the stereo set-up.

My coffee cup and ashtray waited for me
on the glass-topped table, and my heart
went out to them. I said, *Hello, friends,*
or something like that. After all,
this wasn't so bad.
Worse things had happened. This
was even a little funny. I found the ladder.
Took that and leaned it against the house.
Then climbed in the rain to the deck,
swung myself over the railing
and tried the door. Which was locked,
of course. But I looked in just the same
at my desk, some papers, and my chair.
This was the window on the other side
of the desk where I'd raise my eyes
and stare out when I sat at that desk.
This is not like downstairs, I thought.
This is something else.

And it was something to look in like that, unseen,
from the deck. To be there, inside, and not be there.
I don't even think I can talk about it.
I brought my face close to the glass
and imagined myself inside,
sitting at the desk. Looking up
from my work now and again.
Thinking about some other place
and some other time.
The people I had loved then.

I stood there for a minute· in the rain.
Considering myself to be the luckiest of men.
Even though a wave of grief passed through me.
Even though I felt violently ashamed
of the injury I'd done back then.
I bashed that beautiful window.
And stepped back in.

Fred Chappell

Born in 1936 in Canton, North Carolina, Fred Chappell spent his childhood in the mountains of North Carolina. He was educated at Duke University, where he studied under William Blackburn. Since 1964 he has taught at the University of North Carolina at Greensboro. Chappell has published four volumes of poems, beginning in 1971 with *The World Between the Eyes*; *Source* is his latest poetry collection. He has also published five novels, most recently *I Am One of You Forever*. Chappell has received grants from the Rockefeller Foundation and from the National Institute of Arts and Letters, the Bollingen Prize in poetry (with John Ashbery), and a Roanoke-Chowan Poetry Award.

The Virtues

The vices are always hungry for my hands,
But the virtues stay inside their houses like shy brown thrushes.

I feel their presences
Behind the white clapboard walls with all the ugly gingerbread.

They are walking about the dim cool rooms
In handsewn linen dresses.

Is it empty to wish they will come out
To sweep the walks when I stand under the oak across the street?

The virtues are widowed sisters.
No man has been with them for many years.

I believe they are waiting for cataclysm.
They will open their doors

When perfect ruin has taken down this city,
Will wander forth and sift thoughtfully in the hot rubble.

Maxine Chernoff

Maxine Chernoff is a poet, a fiction writer, and the co-editor of *Oink!* She teaches creative writing at Columbia College in Chicago and is a board member of the Poetry Center at the Art Institute of Chicago. *New Faces of 1952* (Ithaca House: 1985) is her fourth book. Chernoff has received two Illinois Arts Council Artist Grants.

A Name

Suppose your parents had called you Dirk. Wouldn't
that be motive enough to commit a heinous crime, just
as Judys always become nurses and Brads, florists? After
the act, your mom would say, "He was always a good
boy. Once on my birthday he gave me one of those roses
stuck in a glass ball. You know, the kind that never
gets soggy"—her Exhibit A. Exhibit B: a surprised
corpse, sharing a last moment of Dirk with the morti-
cian. And Dad would say, "Dirk once won a contest by
spelling the word 'pyrrhic,'" and in his alcohol dream
he sees the infant Dirk, all pink and tinsel, signing his
birth certificate with a knife. Still, Dirk should have
known better. He could tell you that antimony is
Panama's most important product. He remembered
Vasco da Gama and wished him well. Once he'd made
a diorama of the all-American boyhood: a little farm,
cows the size of nails, cottonball sheep, a corncob silo,
but when he signed it Dirk, the crops were blighted by

34

bad faith. Too bad. And don't forget Exhibits C, D, E . . .
The stolen éclair, the zoo caper, the taunting of a certain
Miss W., who smelled of fried onions. It was his parents'
fault. They called him Dirk.

Sotto Voce

Although she's only four, my daughter knows Spanish.
Say *blanco*, she demands, say *negro*. Words are the finest
toys, she tells me with eyes that are arrows. My husband
speaks with the virtuosity of a drummer: *suspiration*,
humidor, *revivify*. Beautiful words float upwards like jets
sewing clouds. If my cat could only speak, it would be
in a shrill, nasal French I wouldn't understand. Lan-
guages wash over me, scratched in cold telephone booths,
tapped on windowpanes. I am sorry to admit that I'm
inventing yet another, in the dark, furtively as one
remembers an obscene old kiss. Just as I am thinking
about it, my daughter shouts *verde*, *verde*. She thinks so
much depends on it—palm trees, parsley, dollar bills—
that I can't disappoint her. Foolish girl, I think, locking
up my new language. Then *verde* dissolves, naked and
bloodless, into the busy air.

Nicholas Christopher

Born in New York City in 1951, Nicholas Christopher was educated at Harvard College. *On Tour with Rita* (Knopf: 1982) is his first collection of poetry. His second collection, *A Short History of the Island of Butterflies*, was recently published by Knopf. *The Soloist* is Christopher's first novel. His honors include the Amy Lowell Travelling Scholarship in 1983, and he is currently leading poetry workshops in New York City.

Lineage

Here's a photograph taken in Manhattan in 1891.
From a rooftop looking south
on the first day of summer.
A man with a cane is smoking in a doorway,
watching a woman alight from a carriage.
A dog is crouched at his heels.
The flags are at half-mast.
In the distance, in Union Square, construction is underway
on another office building,
and some falling bricks just scattered the pigeons.
It was the year before my grandfather was born.
The clock on the bank reads 9:30.
Across from the bank is a theater.
On the sidewalk a vendor is examining a peach

and a policeman is gazing at the sky.
Two boys are rolling a hoop under the marquee.
All of them are dead now.

That same day my great-grandmother was on her honeymoon.
Sitting by the window of the bridal suite
in an Athens hotel—
staring out across the night at the fiery bougainvillea
that rings the Royal Gardens.
Her husband is asleep on the couch
under a thick blue shadow.
She has wrapped his jacket around her shoulders.
She is seventeen years old.
Eight months later she will die in childbirth,
but her son—my grandfather—will survive.
Eventually, he will emigrate and settle in Manhattan.
My father and I will be born there,
and I will write this poem there on a summer day,
on another rooftop.

In the photograph there is also a girl in a hotel window.
She is looking directly at the photographer, through the sunlight.
She is very pale, her eyes are wide,
and she resembles my future wife.
The clock on the bank still reads 9:30,
but it appears that some in the crowd have moved:
the vendor has pocketed the peach
and the man with the dog is crossing the street
and the boys' hoop is lying in the gutter.
The girl in the window has changed, too.
Her face has darkened and her gaze is averted—
as if someone has called to her from across the room.
Across the years.

Amy Clampitt

Born in New Providence, Iowa, Amy Clampitt was educated at Grinnell College. She has published two collections of poetry, *The Kingfisher* (1983) and most recently *What the Light Was Like* (1985). Her poems have appeared in literary magazines since 1978. In 1984 her alma mater awarded her an Honorary Doctorate in Humane Letters. Clampitt's other honors include fellowships from the Guggenheim Foundation and the Academy of American Poets, and an American Academy and Institute of Arts and Letters Award in literature. She currently lives in New York City.

Time

It may be we are in the last days.
Seven hundred years ago to the week,
on the eleventh of December, the kingdom of Wales went under.
Today, the sixth day of the twelfth month of the nineteen hundred
    eighty-second year, according to the current reckoning,
there are roses the size of an obsolete threepenny bit—
one fingernail-pink, the other minute, extravagant crimson—
flanked by masses of sweet alyssum
and one time-exempt purple pansy
on the site of what was formerly the Women's House of Detention
at the triangular intersection of Tenth Street with Greenwich and
    Sixth Avenues,
just back of the old Jefferson Market courthouse
whose tower clock, revived, goes on keeping time.

And I think again of October violets,
of their hardy refusal to adhere to conventional expectation—
so hardy that I've finally ceased to think of it as startling,
this phenomenon which, in fact, I devoted myself in October to
    looking for—
a tame revenant of the blue fire-alarm of the original encounter
    with the evidence,
among the dropped leaves and superannuated grass of the season
    of hickory nuts,
that neither time nor place could be counted on to remain
    self-sufficient,
that you might find yourself slipping back toward the past at any
    moment,
or watch it well up in artesian springs of anachronism,
with the prospect of being drowned in that aperture's abrupt blue,
in that twinkling of an eye, at any moment.
It was November, or near then, I found violets massed at the foot
    of the foundations of the castle of Chepstow,
at the edge of Wales—not any longer, as once, covert, fecklessly
    undermining
that sense of fitness, so fragile that at any moment of one's
    childhood
whatever sense of continuity has not ebbed or been marked for
    demolition
may break like an eggshell, and be overrun from within by the
    albumen of ruin—
their out-of-season purple not any longer hinting at something, but
    announcing it with a flourish:
the entire gorgeous, intractable realm of the forgotten,
the hieratic, the heraldic, the royal, sprung open
at the gouty foot of that anachronism
on the fringes of a kingdom that went under
at or near the downward slope of the thirteenth century. I have
      seen
the artesian spring of the past foam up at the foot of the castle of
    Chepstow

on a day in November, or thereabouts. I have seen a rose the size
   of a perfectly manicured crimson fingernail
alive in a winter that does not arrive, though we plunge again
   toward the solstice.

Suzanne Cleary

Born in 1955 in Binghamton, New York, Suzanne Cleary received a B.A. in history and anthropology from the State University College of New York at Oneonta and an M.A. in creative writing from Washington University. Her poetry has appeared in *MSS*, *The American Poetry Review*, *The Georgia Review*, and *Prairie Schooner*. She won Sotheby's International Poetry Competition in 1982. Cleary has been the Education and Program Director at Philipse Manor Hall since 1983. She is currently completing a poetry manuscript.

The Heart as Dog
for Carita

I
The heart wakes
suddenly
alert, at the foot of their bed.

Its master dreams of a lake.
The woman's hands are curled
as if she is swimming.

The heart is thirsty, and wakes.

II
The heart prowls

across their legs, which glow
like river currents chosen by moonlight.

The heart stands on its four legs
between them. It drinks the darkness
between its master's mouth and her nape.

III
They sleep as if they have slept this way
since before they were born,
as if their child had slept
three seasons in the space his hand cups.

The heart does not understand time.
It does not beg the moonlight to stay
as the woman does, drawing her knees closer.

IV
The heart would end this sleep.
It would lick these faces
and breathe in these ears.

It would whimper for joy.

V
Where is the heart's master? Only his body is here, waiting
for the dawn, for the woman to stir, flinch with dream.
The master is far away, where he cannot shout,
and he has forgotten the heart's name.

If you touch the master's cheek, he feels nothing.

The heart stands guard over this bed.
It will wait, endlessly,
curled into itself.

It is almost the shape of the earth, almost round, having chosen
one kernel of darkness to love until dawn.

VI
In the morning, when the lovers share their dreams
the heart paces the small room, aching

to run
into the day.

Marc Cohen

Born in Brooklyn, New York in 1951, Marc Cohen was raised in Syosset, Long Island. He received a B.A. from the State University of New York at Albany in 1973 and an M.F.A. from Brooklyn College in 1976. He co-edited *Junction* magazine during the year 1974–1975. Cohen's poetry has appeared in several anthologies and in such magazines as *Shenandoah*, *Partisan Review*, *Epoch*, *The Massachusetts Review*, *Denver Quarterly*, *New York Quarterly*, *Oink!*, and *The Bad Henry Review*. He is now seeking publication of his poetry manuscript, *Westwind Cottage*, and he is currently residing in New York City.

Blithe Cabbage

Revision "B" adds a quarter inch slot
to provide clearance.
The art of too much faith, too little Isaac;
using a mistake as the image of an idea.
To provide clearance
has meant a lot to America;
using a mistake as the image of an idea.
The question who killed The Industrial Age
has meant a lot to America.
Blind to river and chronicle the wind sings
the question who killed The Industrial Age.
Some bywords are rich, thin and beautiful.
Blind to river and chronicle the wind sings

an old art of manure that poisons a new knowledge.
Some bywords are rich, thin and beautiful
made iridescent by rain
An old art of manure that poisons a new knowledge,
the blithe cabbage joins purple with green and white
made iridescent by rain.
Smoke lifts from the burning tobacco,
the blithe cabbage joins purple with green and white.
"Let me call you sweetheart, ... "
Smoke lifts from the burning tobacco.
This rim of fire is not refuted, it is snuffed out later.
"Let me call you sweetheart, ... "
Revision "B" adds a quarter inch slot.
This rim of fire is not refuted, it is snuffed out later;
the art of too much faith, too little Isaac.

Jim Daniels

Born in 1956, Jim Daniels grew up in Detroit, Michigan. His first book, *Places/Everyone* (1985), received the inaugural Brittingham Prize in poetry. Most of Daniels' poems center around the life of an auto-plant worker named Digger and have appeared in such magazines as *The Greenfield Review*, *Pulpsmith*, *New Letters*, and *Cimarron Review*. In 1985 he was awarded a National Endowment for the Arts Creative Writing Fellowship. He is currently living in Pittsburgh, Pennsylvania.

#3, Behind Chatham's Supermarket

In the alley behind Chatham's
two boys and an older man stand stained
in aprons, lean against the dumpster smell.

In the field between Chatham's and Delta Drugs
broken glass, candy wrappers, footprints
lie frozen in earth.

Three cigarettes smoke the air.
Across the street, the high school
spills toward them.

The boys pose in faded letter jackets,
playing hooky briefly again, stamp
guns on their belts.

The man is smiling as one boy speaks.
He is watching the back door, measuring distances.
No clues to what has put him here.

If I could, I would watch until the earth thawed,
took in new shapes, shifted with possibility.
What could be a rat moves through the picture.

Lydia Davis

Born in 1947 in Northampton, Massachusetts, Lydia Davis received a B.A. from Barnard College. She has taught at Bard College, Columbia University, and the University of California at San Diego, where she led fiction and translation workshops. Her translations and co-translations include more than twenty titles by Jean-Paul Sartre, Georges Simenon, Maurice Blanchot, Michel Foucault, and others. Her work has appeared in *The Paris Review*, *Fiction International*, and *Harper's*. She has received grants from the National Endowment for the Arts and the Ingram Merrill Foundation. *Break It Down*, her first collection, will be published by Farrar, Straus & Giroux this year.

What She Knew

People did not know what she knew, that she was not really a woman but a man, often a fat man, but more often, probably, an old man. The fact that she was an old man made it hard for her to be a young woman. It was hard for her to talk to a young man, for instance, though the young man was clearly interested in her. She had to ask herself, Why is this young man flirting with this old man?

The Dog Man

A man in our office is really a dog. He does not do well, is slow and clumsy though extremely good-natured. There is also a dog in our town who is really a man and is tormented by his inability to handle things and to express himself and thus cannot be good-natured but is sly and furtive and ashamed of himself. He is hated by everyone and kicked into the corner of the room. Of course that is only one kind of dog who is really a man: another kind of dog who is really a man is like the man who is really a dog in our office, and he does very well because he is really most comfortable as a dog.

David Denny

Born in Lynwood, California in 1960, David Denny received a B.A. in English from California State University, Long Beach, and an M.F.A. in creative writing from the University of Oregon. His poetry has appeared in such literary magazines as *The Beloit Poetry Journal*. He currently lives in northern California.

Holden Caulfield at the Car Wash

1. These old ladys kill me.
   They really do.
   "Fill it up," they'll say,
   without so much as a glance at me.
   Well, I'm about the best
   gas-pumper you ever saw in your life.
   I'm a true madman on the pumps.
   I can set the trigger on high automatic
   and flip it off on the cent.
   I'm a goddamn wizard at pumping gas.
   I really am.
   But what gets me,
   what rattles my coconuts,
   are the biddys who just say,
   "Fill it up."
   Not so much as a glance.
   I'd like to stick my face
   down into theirs sometime and say,

"How 'bout the magic word, lady?
How 'bout, 'fill it up, *please*?' Eh?"
That'd get 'em.
Naw. They'd just think I was
a wise bastard and drive off.
Still, I'd like to try it sometime.

2. Then there are the morons who don't listen.
They pull the car into the wash.
"Put the car in neutral," I say.
"Don't brake or steer."
Some big-shots sit there
in their souped-up Chevys
like they were goddamn A.J. Foyt.
The phonies.
They drive through the wash
at about a hundred miles an hour,
pop their stupid tires,
and try to make out like
it's your fault.
That kills me.
I'm telling you,
the world is full of these guys.
Serves 'em right to get their tires popped.

3. It's raining like crazy
and an old Caddy drives
into the station.
I pull on my goddamn hunting cap
and run like hell to the driver's window.
"A buck's wortha regular," he says.
I get soaked pumping his
lousy dollar's worth,
then he hands me a twenty!
I ask you,
why doesn't the sonuvabitch

put in five or ten bucks?
These people knock me out.
I'm not kidding.
Then he tears out of the lot and
burns the buck's wortha regular
before he reaches the corner.

4. This old guy,
   a regular Adolph Hitler
   (ugly little moustache and all)
   is always spitting tobacco at my feet
   and blabbing about
   how many miles he gets to the gallon.
   He pulls up in a big white Olds
   and says,
   "Fill me up with unleaded."
   I'd love to.
   I really would.
   I can see myself
   grabbing him by the hair,
   yanking back his head,
   cramming the nozzle down his throat
   and filling him up with unleaded.

Toi Derricotte

Born in Detroit, Michigan, Toi Derricotte is a master teacher for the New Jersey State Council on the Arts. She has published two poetry collections, *The Empress of the Death House* (1978) and *Natural Birth* (1982). Her poems appear in such anthologies as *An Introduction to Poetry* (edited by Louis Simpson) and in such magazines as *The Iowa Review*. Derricotte has been guest poet at the Library of Congress and at more than one hundred universities, libraries, and museums throughout the United States. She won the Lucille Medwick Memorial Award from the Poetry Society of America in 1985, and she has received fellowships from the National Endowment for the Arts, the New Jersey State Council on the Arts, and the MacDowell artist colony.

Saturday Night

we come home from the movie, and you head for the t.v.
i peek out of the bathroom to hear you move around in
        there.
i'm screaming: "you're sick, i can't take it anymore.
    you've been with machines all day—computers, t.v.
    you don't want anything to do with me."
you deny this. you had only gone into that room to
        put down your wallet.
i want to kill, am crazed with the smell of my own blood.
"i don't need this. you think i need you like before?"
i hear you in the bathroom cutting your fingernails,

it takes a long time. i wonder if you are on the toilet.
"you're so used to me being the one to need you, it's
   a game. but games can be stopped," i scream,
"games can be stopped."
i grab a magazine and get into bed, flipping through. i
   want to attack until i feel you in my hands, cut
   through to the other side, like diving toward light.
   but i know this never happens; the water gets darker . . .
will you save me? will you reach out your hand and save
   me?
   just one finger on my arm . . .
you pull back the covers and come into bed, gazing up
   at the ceiling.
i want to touch you, but can't move. how can i stay in
   a room too small to stand or sit or lay in—cramped into
   a fetal posture?
i want to threaten until god takes back his lies of
   paradise, till the sun cracks open and lets us die.
we are packed in a frame bed like a child's wagon in
   the middle of a tornado.
"games can be stopped," i repeat, softly. "but it hurts."

"i am so lonely," i say. "so lonely."

Tom Disch

Born in Des Moines, Iowa in 1942, Tom Disch has lived in New York since 1956. In addition to six collections of poetry, he has published twelve novels, several short story collections, children's books, libretti, and interactive software. His *ABCDEFG HIJKLM NPOQRST UVWXYZ* (1981), *Burn This* (1982), and *Here I Am, There You Are, Where You Were* (1984) will be brought out by Doubleday in a single-volume collection later this year.

The Size of the World

To say it is enormous, or to search the thesaurus
For synonyms to its immensity will not express
The size of it. It dwarfs all our opinions
And knowledge, and even when we try to expand
Our vocabulary to take in the latest large
Idea, such as superstrings or ecology
Or the transcending of this or that category,
We are only inventing new conventions.
Something is left out in even the best new schema:
There is no room for happiness
Or the Holy Family on Xmas Eve
Or the price of eggs or something else so significant
That without it all the rest is vanity.
Nor is there any wisdom in such an admission;
It is as a watercolour of the ocean
To the ocean itself. But this can be a source

Of joy, or, lacking that, of a sweet and needful
Self-deception, a safety exit
To practical faith, not one connected
To what may be known but only to what may not.
This is the realm poetry particularly
Inhabits, the teasing out of thought
Into pleasing shapes, coiffing the minds
Of a happy few to some provisory accommodation
To their ignorance—without euphoria,
Without unfounded hope, and yet enchanted.
Oh, it is a realm isolate as Moctezuma's,
And, some have said, forlorn. But vivider,
For all that, than the actual universe
In which we bulk so small, and which impinges
Every split-second even on these complacent
Maunderings, suggesting other combinations,
More refined adaptions to the fact
Of all facts, the set of all sets, the sum
Of all summery days, when the sun shines
With Platonic brightness and the mind is inclined
To lazily number the ways I love you, and the cause
Of it: To wit, because you're fair, because
We've been together since the dawn of time, because
You're so fine a backseat driver, or because
You've got a way with words mine *and* yours.
By such means—poetry, love, what have you—
The universe can be contained, the world
Reduced to a manageable mass
Where superstrings may coexist
With the atoms of Democritus, though we know
All the while the world is larger
Than all these transcripts of our idle chatter.
Some things matter more than others: mothers
More than Coca-Cola, pigeons more than fleas.
Yet even these neglected categories
May abound in unthought possibilities.

Life's so rich, and life's only a part of it:
There are, as well, minerals and large machines,
Bricks and various gases—and, if *The Times* is right,
Six entirely new dimensions, ten
In all, and we may be, in every one,
A kind of sun unto our constituent
Genes, and our Roy Rogers too, a meaty
Stew of recombinant nuances;
Cities built, and histories, meals cooked,
Books read, scenes viewed, drawers opened and closed,
Glimpsed lovelinesses and horrors, which in
Some larger perspective, some stricter mind's
Accounting, are as the blow that ended
Tamburlaine and not of immediate importance.
Though, who knows, without some particular
Forgotten warlord we might not be here to share
This evanescing afternoon of broken-
Bottled pavements and friendly endlessness,
Friendly because no one cares. So life's a scream,
So what? What are we doing when we talk
Like this, unlistened to, a ballpoint
Pressed against the ruled paper's tenderness?

---

superstrings: particles viewed not as being composed of quarks but as a sequence of
points in a ten-dimension universe.

Stephen Dobyns

Born in Orange, New Jersey in 1941, Stephen Dobyns is a novelist, poet, and essayist. His first book of poems, *Concurring Beasts* (Atheneum: 1972), was the Lamont Selection of the Academy of American Poets. Dobyns has since published five more poetry collections, most recently *Cemetery Nights* (Viking: 1987). He has received a Guggenheim Fellowship and two National Endowment for the Arts Fellowships. Dobyns currently teaches in the M.F.A. writing program at Warren Wilson College.

The Face in the Ceiling

A man comes home to find his wife in bed
with the milkman. They're really going at it.
The man yanks the milkman off by his heels
so his chin hits the floor. Then he gets his gun.
It looks like trouble for all concerned.
Why is modern life so complicated?
The wife and milkman scramble into their clothes.
The man makes them sit at the kitchen table,
takes all but one bullet out of the gun,
then spins the cylinder. We'll let fate decide,
he says. For the sake of symmetry, he gets their
mongrel dog and makes him sit at the table as well.
The dog is glad to oblige but fears the worst.
North, south, east, west, says the man, who's the one
that God likes best? He puts the gun to his head

and pulls the trigger. Click. Whew, what a relief.
Spinning the cylinder, he aims the gun at his wife.
North, south, east, west, he says and again pulls
the trigger. Another click. He spins the cylinder
and aims at the milkman. North, south, east, west.
A third click. He points the gun at the dog who is
scratching nervously at his collar. North, south,
east, west, who do you think God likes best?
The man pulls the trigger. Bang! He's killed the dog.
Good grief, says the wife, he was just a pup.
They look down at the sprawled body of the dog
and are so struck by the mean-spiritedness
of the world's tricks that they can do nothing
but go out for a pizza and something to drink.
When they have finished eating, the man says,
You take my wife home, I'm sorry I was selfish.
And the milkman says, No, you take her home,
I'm sorry I was greedy. And the wife says,
Let's all go home together. A little later
they are lying side by side on the double bed
completely dressed and shyly holding hands.
They stare up at the ceiling where they think
they see God's face in the ridges of shadow,
the swirls of plaster and paint. It looks like
the kid who first punched me in the nose,
says the husband. It looks like the fellow
who fired me from my first job, says the milkman.
And the wife remembers once as a child
a man who called her over to his car,
and opening the door she saw he was naked
from his waist down to his red sneakers.
What makes you think that God likes anyone?
asks the wife. Wide awake, the three of them
stare at the ceiling trying to define the kind
of face they find there until the sun comes up
and pushes away the shadow and then it no longer

matters whether the face is good or evil, generous
or small minded. So they get up, feeling sheepish,
and don't look at each other as they wash and
brush their teeth and drink a cup of coffee,
then go out and make their way in the world,
neither too badly nor too well as is the case
with compromises, sneaking along walls, dashing
across streets. You think it is nothing to risk
your life every day of the great struggle until
what you hold most precious is torn from you?
How loudly the traffic roars, how ferociously
the great machines bear down upon them
and how courageous it is for them to be there.

Edward Field

Born in 1924, Edward Field was educated at New York University and served in the U.S. Air Force during World War II. His first book of poetry, *Stand Up, Friend, with Me*, won the Lamont Poetry Selection Award in 1963; his other poetry collections include *A Full Heart* and *Stars in My Eyes*. Field has edited anthologies and has translated Eskimo poetry.

Night Song

When I get up in the night to pee
I'm no longer myself but my father—

that's when I feel most like him,
an old man going to the bathroom,

joyless, miserable, grim—
even my urine smells like him.

Oh, I do not want to be like him.

It's as if he's crawled under my skin,
irritating me there, working deeper in.

It is because we share one skin?
Oh, how I dislike in the night becoming him.

To write this down I turn on the light
and waking, you ask what's wrong.
Nothing, I answer, It's all right,
and by speaking, become myself again.

But I'm irrevocably awake and tossing till dawn,
thinking of every stupid thing I've ever done,
and though I have to desperately, not getting up to pee—
Oh, how I hate it, hate it, being me.

Gary Gildner

Born in West Branch, Michigan in 1938, Gary Gildner received a B.A. in journalism and an M.A. in comparative literature from Michigan State University. A poet and fiction writer, Gildner has published eight books of poetry, most recently *Blue Like the Heavens* in 1984. *The Crush*, a collection of stories, was published in 1983. Two more books are forthcoming in 1987: a second collection of stories, *A Week in South Dakota*, and a novel, *The Second Bridge*. He has won many awards including the Robert Frost Fellowship, the William Carlos Williams Poetry Prize, the Theodore Roethke Poetry Prize, two National Endowment for the Arts Fellowships, and a Pushcart Prize. Gildner has lived in Mexico and France, and he has taught at Drake University and Reed College. He is currently teaching at his alma mater.

Sometimes We Throw Things
in the Car, Fast

and take off, hurt, mad, kissing it all good-bye.
Most of us, maybe, have done that. I knew a woman once
threw an ice bucket, ten sweatshirts, and her high school
annual in the car, ripped out of the driveway spitting
gravel and didn't pull over until she heard a lone
killdeer cry on a farmer's fence post. I loved that woman.
I loved her crooked toes and her sweet seven-grain
bread fresh from the oven, and I loved the good fit

the front of my knees made with the backs of hers.
And much more. But she took off. I know why

she grabbed the sweatshirts, winter or summer
that's almost all she wears, and the ice bucket
(a gift from her maiden Aunt Jelly) she used for
cattails, her favorite quote flowers. But why that ugly
purple annual I'll never know—remembering high school
made her wince and shudder, and the annual's pompous
name, *Veritas*, she hated. The truth is, I don't know
if a killdeer stopped her or not. I only know
she likes their lonesome song, so every time
I hear one I imagine she had to stop. Maybe afraid
she also picked up the annual, read some gems

her classmates had penned in blues and greens
beside their pictures—as she did for me
one New Year's Eve when we polished off a bottle of cognac
in front of the fire, remembering things—remember the swell
times in Mr. Six's World Lit, and stay as sweet as you are,
and good luck next year with your fabulous modeling career!
The modeling line gave her the giggles—made her say Wow,
that was close. Then she read something that made her say Oh.
And shake her head. Little Timmy Noonan, she said, touching
his small jerky script. I saw it. You are perfect, he wrote,

and appeared to wish he could disappear through his collar.
Maybe she didn't read the annual. Maybe she just looked
at some black cattle standing at ease in the pasture,
their moony eyes slowly turning to face her. No,
that's awful. The crooked silo full of holes and all
those swallows perched around the rim like wicked spitcurls
are no good either. Little Timmy Noonan never
knew her, she said. No one did. She left. And jerky
words, moony cattle, silos, or listening hard

to birds calling up their own worlds
beside the road—none of that will bring her back.

Louise Glück

Louise Glück was born in New York City in 1943. She attended
Sarah Lawrence College and Columbia University, where she
studied under Stanley Kunitz. Her first book, *Firstborn*, was
published when she was twenty years old. Since that time she has
published *The House on the Marshland* (1975), *Descending Figure*
(1980), and *The Triumph of Achilles* (1985). Among her honors are
grants from the Guggenheim Foundation, the Rockefeller Founda-
tion, and the National Endowment for the Arts. She was also the
recipient of the Academy of American Poets Prize in 1966 and the
Eunize Tietjens Memorial Prize in 1971. Most recently Glück
received the 1985 National Book Critics Circle Award for *The
Triumph of Achilles*. She has taught at Columbia University and at
the University of Virginia. Presently she is living in Vermont and is
teaching at Williams College.

Summer

Remember the days of our first happiness,
how strong we were, how dazed by passion,
lying all day, then all night in the narrow bed,
sleeping there, eating there too: it was summer,
it seemed everything had ripened
at once. And so hot we lay completely uncovered.
Sometimes the wind rose; a willow brushed the window.

But we were lost in a way, didn't you feel that?
The bed was like a raft; I felt us drifting
far from our natures, toward a place where we'd discover
    nothing.
First the sun, then the moon, in fragments,
shone through the willow.
Things anyone could see.

Then the circles closed. Slowly the nights grew cool;
the pendant leaves of the willow
yellowed and fell. And in each of us began
a deep isolation, though we never spoke of this,
of the absence of regret.
We were artists again, my husband.
We could resume the journey.

5. Night Song, fr. Marathon

Look up into the light of the lantern.
Don't you see? The calm of darkness
is the horror of Heaven.

We've been apart too long, too painfully separated.
How can you bear to dream,
to give up watching? I think you must be dreaming,
your face is full of mild expectancy.

I need to wake you, to remind you that there isn't a future.
That's why we're free. And now some weakness in me
has been cured forever, so I'm not compelled
to close my eyes, to go back, to rectify—

The beach is still; the sea, cleansed of its superfluous life,
opaque, rocklike. In mounds, in vegetal clusters,
seabirds sleep on the jetty. Terns, assassins—

You're tired; I can see that.
We're both tired, we have acted a great drama.
Even our hands are cold, that were like kindling.
Our clothes are scattered on the sand; strangely enough,
they never turned to ashes.

I have to tell you what I've learned, that I know now
what happens to the dreamers.
They don't feel it when they change. One day
they wake, they dress, they are old.

Tonight I'm not afraid
to feel the revolutions. How can you want sleep
when passion gives you that peace?
You're like me tonight, one of the lucky ones.
You'll get what you want. You'll get your oblivion.

Lucinda Grealy

Born in Ireland in 1963, Lucinda Grealy has lived in New York since 1967. She received her B.A. from Sarah Lawrence College in 1985 and is currently studying at the Iowa Writers' Workshop. Her poems have appeared in *Ploughshares* and *Intro 14*. She has been awarded two Academy of American Poets Prizes.

Ferrying horses

This is only a short trip
but the horses don't know that
blindfolded beneath the deck.
They stand tense and steaming,
I know their eyes are walled and bright
beneath the cloth.
Their hard breathing is my asking
what should I do? and telling myself nothing.
The ship's horn, a sudden shift;
it doesn't take much to scare them
and the dropped glass thing that does
brings a sudden bolt, the grabbing
of an ear and my digging fingers in a neck.
The mare, a dun, drags me along
like everything I won't let go of.
My face is forced next to hers
and for fifty seconds my life
is the purple I see in her nostril.

When it's over we're topside in the sunlight
and the ship's mate keeps asking Trouble?,
but I'm still thinking of being a color,
how everything became so sharp, so different.
Sound is another name for fear to these animals,
just as this ship is his own heart
to the captain, and for the men
working on dock the days are rope
and the words nearly over.
On shore there's a woman whose life
is beneath her window each warm night,
a person's wanting her to forget everything
and come out. She's the shade of red
lonely women paint their walls.

Linda Gregg

Born in Suffern, New York in 1942, Linda Gregg grew up in northern California. She received her B.A. and her M.A. from San Francisco State University. She has taught poetry at the University of Tucson, the Napa Valley Poetry Conference at Napa Valley College, and at the "Gathering of Poets" at Louisiana State University. Her honors include the Frank Stanford Memorial Prize, First Prize of the Poetry Society of America, and a Guggenheim Fellowship in 1983. Gregg's first book, *Too Bright to See*, was published in 1981, and her poetry appears regularly in literary magazines.

Late Afternoon in California

We lived in the country when I was small.
I tried to make houses in the bay trees
and the live oaks, but it always got dark
and time for supper. Now my father is dead
and his name faded to a bruise. Mother
is on the porch reading an old letter of his
to prove he did not care about me. She says
it was because I was sexual as a child.
I remind her I always cut my hair short
and wore only boys' clothing. There was
something about the way you walked she says
and goes inside, saying there is nothing
to eat and she is tired of cooking.

Marilyn Hacker

Born in New York City in 1942, Marilyn Hacker was educated at the Bronx High School of Science and at Washington Square College, New York University. She has been a mail sorter, a teacher, an editor, and an antiquarian bookseller. Her first book, *Presentation Piece* (1974), was the Lamont Selection of the Academy of American Poets and won the National Book Award in 1975. Of her six volumes of poetry, *Love, Death, and the Changing of the Seasons* (Arbor House: 1986) is the most recent. She currently edits the feminist literary magazine *13th Moon*.

Nights of 1964–66: The Old Reliable

The laughing soldiers fought to their defeat
       James Fenton, "In a Notebook"

White decorators interested in art,
Black file clerks with theatrical ambitions,
kids making pharmaceutical revisions
in journals Comp. instructors urged they start,
the part-Cherokee teenage genius—maybe—
the secretary who hung out with fairies,
the copywriter wanting to know, where is
my husband? the soprano with the baby,
all drank draft beer or lethal sweet Manhattans
or improvised concoctions with tequila
in summer, when, from Third Street, we could feel a
night breeze waft in whose fragrances were Latin.

The place was run by Polish refugees:
squat Margie, gaunt Speedy—whose sobriquet
transliterated what? He'd brought his play
from Lodz. After a while, we guessed Margie's
illiteracy was why *he* cashed checks
and *she* perched near the threshhold to ban pros,
the underage, the fugitive, and those
arrayed impertinently to their sex.
The bar was talk and cruising; in the back
room, we danced: Martha and the Vandellas,
Smokey and the Miracles; while sellers
and buyers changed crisp tens for smoke and smack.
Some came in after work, some after supper,
plumage replenished to meet who knew who.
Margie, behind the bar, dished up beef stew.
On weeknights, you could always find an upper
to speed you to your desk, and drink till four.
Loosened by booze, we drifted, on the ripples
of Motown, home in new couples, or triples,
were back at dusk, with I.D.'s, at the door.
Bill was my roommate, Russell drank with me,
although they were a dozen years my seniors.
I walked off with the eighteen-year-old genius
—an Older Woman, barely twenty-three.
Link was new as Rimbaud, but better-looking,
North Beach bar *paideon* of doomed Jack Spicer,
like Russell, our two-meter artificer,
a Corvo whose *ecclesia* was cooking.
Bill and Russell were painters. Bill had been
a monk in Kyoto. Stoned, we sketched together,
till he discovered poppers and black leather
and Zen consented to new discipline.
We shared my Sixth Street flat with a morose
cat, an arch cat, and pot-plants we pruned daily.
His boyfriend had left him for an Israeli
dancer; my husband was on Mykonos.

Russell loved Harold who was Black and bad,
and lavished on him dinners "meant for men"
like Escoffier and Brillat-Savarin.
Staunch blond Dora made rice. When she had
tucked in the twins, six flights of tenement
stairs they'd descend, elevenish, and stroll
down Third Street, desultory night patrol
gone mauve and green under the virulent
streetlights, to the bar, where Bill and I
(if we'd not come to dinner), Link, and Lew,
and Betty had already had a few.
One sweatsoaked night in pitiless July,
wedged on booth-benches of cracked Naugahyde,
we planned a literary magazine
where North Beach met the Lower East Side scene.
We could have called it, *When Worlds Collide*.
Dora was gone, "in case the children wake up."
Link lightly had decamped with someone else
—the German engineer? Or was he Bill's?
Russell's stooped *Vale* brushed my absent makeup.
Armed children spared us home, our good-night hugs
laisser-passer. We railed against the war.
Soon, some of us bussed South with SNCC and CORE.
Soon, some of us got busted dealing drugs.
The file clerks took exams and forged ahead.
The decorators' kitchens blazed persimmon.
The secretary started kissing women,
and so did I, and my three friends are dead.

James Hazard

Born in 1935 and raised in Whiting, Indiana, James Hazard received a B.A. from Northwestern University and an M.A. from the University of Connecticut. He currently teaches at the University of Wisconsin in Milwaukee. A jazz aficionado, Hazard is now working on a book of poetry that is designed as a tribute to Hoagy Carmichael. His fifth book, *New Year's Eve in Whiting, Indiana* (Main Street Publishing: 1985), won the Council of Wisconsin Writers Best Book Award.

Beyond the Last Straw in Whiting, Indiana

They came back to work on Monday. They stayed
married. They talked to their kids again
and didn't get it right, again. They punched in
and all the rest, how many years after they
swore never again. How many years of work orders
after the last one, last straw, that drove
them permanently drunk or crazy or silent or
humorous or violent or religious or polite or
tool-stealing or hobby-crazed or queer for
summer job schoolboys and girlie mags or alive
only two weeks per summer on some chain
"O Lakes" they bought artificial baits for
fifty weeks a year? Outright suicide was just
about unheard of, as was murder, done outright.
Beyond the last straw comes this numb after

life. You are your own widow, making the most
of it, most of the time, mournful or plucky.
Amazed at how life does not give a shit for you,
you and it go on. You go to all the funerals,
remember yourself on the team or in the war.
You look at the pictures. You decide, like
a widow, to keep his (your) clothes in the closet
one more week and then, and then, . . . Weekends
get chancier and chancier. "Do you know
where your father is," my mother asked. "No."
"Drunk," she said, as if drunk was a place.
He'd left the Elks Club and went, drunk, on
a bus to Chicago, where we'd moved from.
He was asleep at our landlord's apartment.
Saturday afternoon that was. He came home
sober on Sunday, and it never happened again.
He lived another twenty years, died a month
after retirement, and Saturday after Saturday
it never happened again.

Good Lake Michigan

In Whiting, Indiana, it is the edge of town.
The next land straight east is Michigan.
In the Twenties it froze all across. My father
told about a man who walked it. He took
canned goods and built a fire, like Jack London.
We always said about the Lake, it kept us safe
from tornados, would swallow them up into all
its space before they touched us. One ripped down
a Hundred-fifteenth Street and took garages
with it. "Phew! Think what it'd been if we didn't
have the Lake," we said. Summer nights, everyone
sat out and waited on front steps for the Lake
to do what it did best of all. The kids played
Mother Made a Chocolate Cake in the dark and maybe
a radio would be up to a front room screen
with the White Sox game. Some time, around ten
usually, you'd hear it start. Or just see it and
someone would run up and turn the radio down, to hear
it better. Up at the tips of the elms you'd hear it first:
leaves sounded like lucky, paper tickets; a first
breeze entered, like a hand that picks the big number.
The whole town had sat waiting. Now the whole town
stood, and took big breaths. It was time to go in.
The wind had shifted. It was cool enough to sleep
now. The good Lake, that has taken away all those
tornados, gave us now our cool, summer breath.

Michael Heller

Born in New York City in 1937, Michael Heller received a B.S. in engineering from Rennselaer Polytechnic Institute and an M.A. in poetics from New York University. Of his four books of poetry, *Knowledge* (Sun: 1980) is the most recent. A poet and critic, his work has appeared in such magazines as *The Paris Review*, *Conjunctions*, *Harper's*, *New Letters*, *The American Poetry Review*, and *The New York Times Book Review*. He has lectured, taught, and read at several colleges and universities. Heller is currently the U.S. editor of *Origin* and is on the advisory board of *Pequod*. In 1986, he received a Summer Seminar Grant from the National Endowment for the Humanities.

For Uncle Nat

I'm walking down 20th Street with a friend
When a man beckons to me from the doorway
Of Congregation Zichron Moshe. "May I,"
He says to my companion, "borrow this
Jewish gentleman for a moment?" I follow
The man inside, down the carpeted aisle,
Where at the front, resplendent in
Polished wood and gold, stands
The as yet unopened Ark.

Now the doors slide back, an unfolded
Promissory note, and for a moment,

I stand as one among the necessary ten.
The braided cloth, the silver mounted
On the scrolls, even the green of the palm
Fronds placed about the room, such hope
Which breaks against my unbeliever's life.

So I ask, Nat, may I borrow you, for a moment,
To make a necessary two? Last time we lunched,
Enclaved in a deli, in the dim light, I saw
A bit of my father's face in yours. Not to make
Too much of it, but I know history
Stamps and restamps the Jew; our ways
Are rife with only momentary deliverance.
May I borrow you for a moment, Nat. We'll celebrate
By twos, the world's an Ark. We'll talk in slant,
American accent to code the hidden language of the Word.

Robert Hershon

Robert Hershon was born in Brooklyn, New York, in 1936. He is the director of The Print Center, Inc., and the co-editor of Hanging Loose Press and *Hanging Loose* magazine. His work has appeared in several anthologies and in magazines such as *Sun*, *Poetry Northwest*, and *Poetry Now*. The most recent of his nine collections of poetry is *How to Ride on the Woodlawn Express*. Hershon has received fellowships from the National Endowment for the Arts and the Creative Artists Public Service Program.

I Tell My Mother's Daydream
for Maureen Owen

i have stopped writing
those poems
instead i have written
a novel
it is a smash hit
and "they" made it into a movie
and it is a smash hit
and then "it was made" into
a musical
and it was a smash hit
and the musical into another
movie and a novelization of
that and a TV series that starts
tonight and never ends

and now my mother and i are
walking toward johnny carson
and he is telling her she
can't possibly be old enough
to be my mother

Edward Hirsch

Born in Chicago in 1950, Edward Hirsch was educated at Grinnell College and at the University of Pennsylvania. His first book of poems, *For the Sleepwalkers* (Knopf: 1981), was nominated for a National Book Critics Circle Award. The recipient of fellowships from the Ingram Merrill Foundation, the Academy of American Poets, and the National Endowment for the Arts, Hirsch is an instructor at Wayne State University.

My Grandmother's Bed

How she pulled it out of the wall
To my amazement. How it rattled and
Creaked, how it sagged in the middle
And smelled like a used-clothing store.
I was ecstatic to be sleeping on wheels!

It rolled when I moved; it trembled
When she climbed under the covers
In her flannel nightgown, kissing me
Softly on the head, turning her back.
Soon I could hear her snoring next to me—

Her clogged breath roaring in my ears,
Filling her tiny apartment like the ocean,
Until I, too, finally swayed and slept,

While a radiator hissed in the corner
And traffic droned on Lawrence Avenue . . .

I woke up to the color of light pouring
Through the windows, the odor of soup
Simmering in the kitchen, my grandmother's
Face. It felt good to be ashore again
After sleeping on rocky, unfamiliar waves.

I loved to help her straighten the sheets
And lift the Murphy back into the wall.
It was like putting the night away
When we closed the wooden doors again
And her bed disappeared without a trace.

Allen Hoey

Born in Kingston, New York, Allen Hoey received a B.A. from the
State University College at Potsdam, New York in 1974, and an
M.A. and a D.A. from Syracuse University. He has taught at
Syracuse University and Le Moyne College, and he is currently an
assistant professor in the writing program at Ithaca College. Hoey is
founder, publisher, and editor of Tamarack Editions, a small poetry
press established in 1978. Chapbooks of his own work include *New
Year* (Liberty Street: 1986), *Work the Tongue Could Understand*
(State Street: 1986), and *Cedar Light* (Street Press: 1980). *A Fire in
the Cold House of Being*, his first full-length poetry collection, will
be published by the Walt Whitman Center as part of the Camden
Poetry Award. He has also won the American Poets Prize.

Toil

It's certain there is no fine thing
Since Adam's fall but needs much labouring.
—W.B. Yeats

I.

Where I grew up men's hands were not stained brown
digging potatoes, reaping wheat or corn,
or spading peat from bogs to keep them warm.
Brick dust rouged skin raw; the cement plant ground
a fine gray silt in skin, which fell around
a couple miles on houses, too. What form

their corn and barley took was bottled, more
to cut the taste of grime at first than pound
the work from mind. When he got home, he toiled,
after he shed his working clothes—as though
that dirt might somehow blight the cleaner soil—
in his small garden. My father turned his hand
to peas and squash, but most he loved tomatoes:
their taste a work his tongue could understand.

II.

Their taste a work my tongue could understand,
I thought: transforming bread to body, wine
to Christ's bright blood inside. The pastor's hand,
raised like a traffic cop's in black, divine
conductor of our symphony of souls,
made magic with a simple sign; bland bread
become as honeyed baklava unfolded
on tongues then liquored with a holy mead
of song. Broad vowels and breaded consonants,
such work would raise a sweat on any twelve-
year-old's first communion. With God's consent
all miracles are prefaced; and ourselves—
we learn to scoff at loaves and fishes, think
all water turned to wine unfit to drink.

III.

All water turned to wine unfit to drink,
and whether changed by human hand or turned
blood on the tongue no matter. What we learn
is how the sugar's work, without our thinking,
becomes our own, our staple—fluid link
in a dim chain of conversations burned

away once off the tongue. It's work. You yearn
for quenching beer, a sip with meals of pink
chablis or Liebfraumilch. You stick to tea
or coffee, ginger ale at bars and no
communion. Years it's been and still talk veers
to drunken episodes, how many beers
you used to put away and drive to see,
in some abandoned field, dawn's bloody show.

IV.

In some abandoned field, dawn's bloody show
lights up a second growth of pine and ash
already poking through neglected rows
where corn once swayed; a few runt stalks, the last
departing geese had strewn, make their last stand.
It's not been long—two generations past—
this land was tilled. Stones reaped and piled by hand
to mark division; some remain, as Frost
has written, slowly claiming back the land
as though they crawled out on their own. We've lost.
But lost not much but fathers' sweat—and not
our fathers, truth be known—if we can just
avoid the tractors' gnawing thirst for lots
to turn to asphalt parks and tract-home plots.

V.

To turn to asphalt parks and tract-home plots:
our fathers coached us in their dreams. Degree
in hand, we'd stride through life, they believed, free
of sweat; our soft hands show how far our lot
has come from toil. Most days, I lean, all hot
and bothered by a misplaced comma, "we"

misused for ''us,'' across a desk and try
late mornings working up a sweat to blot
boredom by running. My pen's no plough, red
ink not my life's blood to spill on essays
concerning drinking age and draft or gun
control or silly pets. I'd will my son
more balance in his life, more light, the grace
to face each morning's darkness without dread.

     VI.

To face each morning's darkness without dread,
a little grace provides a greater stay
than coffee. Bright-eyed, my son leaps from bed
prepared, though unaware, to meet the day's
great challenge: getting through the day. He sways
where monkey bars give way to air, his sweat
the product of commingled work and play,
and skins the cat with awkward ease, his death
a father's fear. My mother fought each breath
deep, her heart stopped, her mind numbed to our words.
In the other room I built, my son slept
through the paramedics. What sounds he heard
across the hall while they labored to revive
life stemmed within, he'll hold close while alive.

     VII.

Life stems within; held close while I'm alive
the kicks against my hand, my back in sleep.
What gardener ever felt such thrashing deep
in soil he'd planted? First our son: her heave
love's labor at its hardest best, work scribed
in joy, and now this other soon to keep

us sleepless, trying love our hearts will reap
before our hands are ready. Will it thrive?
We'll do our best. We are not gardeners, though
the metaphor is tempting; life's not ground
cowdung can richen, spading ease, or hoeing
bring to fruit. Sweat, yes, as though sun burned
hard on our shoulders, colorless but earned.
Where I grew up men's hands were not stained brown.

                              for my father

Linda Hogan

Born in Denver, Colorado in 1947, and raised on Chickasaw Indian territory in Oklahoma, Linda Hogan received an M.A. in English and creative writing from the University of Colorado. She has taught American Indian literature and creative writing at several colleges and has also given many readings, lectures, and workshops. Hogan has published four books of poetry, and her work often appears in such literary magazines as *The Greenfield Review* and *Conditions*.

Saint Coyote

St. Coyote passed over the highway.
His shadow laid down
in headlights,
yellow eyes.
His fur breathed
in busy suburbs where children kneel
with lights dark as shut eyes.

Another world crosses the streets.
Houses vanish.
Square windows are dark
secrets in the ruins.
Shutters wear out
beating on walls.

Luminous savior
wise to traps
eyes shining like the electric bones
of street lamps,
I heard him last night.
He threw a rock in water
and people followed.
I heard him
beneath a tree, singing
to the disappearing moon
that walks on water
and telling it lies about people.

That saint,
always gambling,
crossing dark streets
walking among skin and shadow,
always lying
about who created death and light.

Jonathan Holden

Born in 1941, Jonathan Holden was educated at Oberlin College, San Francisco State University, and the University of Colorado. *Design for a House* (University of Missouri Press: 1972) was his first book and was the winner of the Devins Award. *Leverage* (University Press of Virginia: 1982) won the Associated Writing Programs Award Series for Poetry. In 1984 Carnegie-Mellon published Holden's latest book, *Falling from Stardom*. Holden is a noted scholar whose critical work includes the essay collection *Rhetoric of the Contemporary Lyric* and a study of the poet William Stafford. He currently teaches at Kansas State University.

Sex Without Love
For X.

If evil had style
it might well resemble
those pointless experiments
we used to set up and run
with our legs and our hands
and our mouths between two
and four p.m. while our kids
were swimming in the public pool
and our wives, or husbands,
were somewhere else—
an hour when nobody wanted
to move, the heat

had gone breathless, slack
as if the afternoon
had been punched in the stomach,
a victim of what we'd coolly
decided to do. There might
be the nagging of a single mower.
At last even that would die
in the heat. We could catch
a rumor of thunder in the hills—
a signal, like the smirk
of swallowed amusement you'd slip
my direction by raising just
slightly your eyebrows as much
as to ask, *Well? Shall we?*
Its style might well resemble
the wholly gratuitous gear
we would then shift down to
as deliberately we would undress,
our eyes wide open, without
compromise, curious to observe what
a body might be up to next
on such a hopeless afternoon,
just barely affection
enough—a pinch of salt—
to produce that sigh, when
for a lucky moment or so
curiosity can be mistaken
for enthusiasm and we learn
what we already know.

Garrett Kaoru Hongo

Garrett Kaoru Hongo was born in Volcano, Hawaii, in 1951 and grew up in Oahu and Los Angeles. Graduating with honors from Pomona College, he studied at the University of Michigan and received an M.F.A. from the University of California at Irvine. Hongo, an assistant professor of English at the University of Missouri, is also a poetry editor at *The Missouri Review*. His poetry has appeared in *The New Yorker*, *Antaeus*, *Field*, and *The Nation*. Hongo has received the Thomas J. Watson Travelling Fellowship (to Japan), the Hopwood Prize for Poetry, the Discovery/*The Nation* Award from the Poetry Center at the 92nd Street Y, and a National Endowment for the Arts Creative Writing Fellowship. *Yellow Light* is the title of his first book.

Morro Rock
for M.J.

       a Thirties blue fedora
slouching through thick China fog off the Pacific;
or, in bright sun, the grey colt
romping in curls of surf, the wash
at its heels, foam breaking against the slate chest;
Duchamp-Villon's horse stolen from its museum
and spray-painted camouflage green,
sliding from the junker pickup
speeding along Highway One, bouncing from its crate
as it slams across asphalt and the gravel shoulder,

at rest, finally, in the cold sand,
nose awash in running tide,
some huge and abandoned engine
stripped from its hot car,
salvage in the sea's green oil,
churning still in the vicious pistons of surf.

I remember best stories in which it figures
as centerpiece or sublime backdrop:
the great albacore run of the Sixties,
men in fraying mackinaws stained with blood
crammed thick as D-Day on the decks
of an excursion or half-day boat
chugging slowly through light fog,
slicks belowdecks, poles high-masted,
a small denuded forest on the sea's false winter,
maybe a thousand fish iced in the hold,
the coast in sight, harbor invisible
except for the black bead of the Rock,
a notched landfall, eloquent on the horizon.

Or the time I played Weston with it,
forcing my father to drive north one day,
up the coast through patchy fog to the Bay.
We stopped at an overlook
snarling with brush and bunches of iceplant,
and he chose the shot, setting the tripod,
while I fiddled with filmpacks
and tested the cloth shutter in the car.
We waited an hour for the fog to be right—
the Rock emerging from it, finally,
a black clipper from the sea.

And I knew a girl once
who lived near there,
and whom I'd visit,

hitching north, needing her still.
She was the first I'd known
who could sit, oblivious,
still in her long shift,
pull both knees to her arms,
and rock gently in the sand
while a thin film of sea washed around her.
I'd stand barefoot in the foam
while the ocean percolated around us,
and toss wet handfuls of sand
towards the combers, empty of feeling.
The Rock filled the space behind us.

Sometimes though,
it's successful lovers I recall,
the battered myth of my teens,
a cheap tale told over bonfires
snapping with kelp and whistling driftwood.
They were young too,
or old beyond counting,
a bachelor Abraham and maidenly Sarah
working their poor farms
on opposite ends of the cove.

They saw each other Sundays at church,
sold raffle tickets and donated specialties
to the annual charity auction—
he volunteered lessons in pier fishing,
she, a picnic lunch in the park by the dunes.
Shyly at first, then with humor and verve,
they bid for each other, waving off competitors.
There was a season of courtship—
football games, holiday dinners together,
a New Year's Eve with foreign champagne
and Glenn Miller records on the hi-fi.
By the next spring, they were making love,

discreetly at first, then, finding the gods
in each other, fierce as teenagers
parked by the Rock, they'd kiss openly,
sprawl over each other on blankets at the Esplanade,
ignoring first the whispers, then the minister's call
and letters of petition from the neighbors.
Before the police could come,
after indecent afternoons under the pier,
riders in pickups came,
hooded like hanged men or cowled in ski masks.
There were women too, undisguised
in their housedresses but keening in the night
as they assembled, crowlike, by the farmshack.
No gunfire, the lovers were killed with stones,
with the snapped limbs of beach oak
and a quick, purging fire of hate.

Before death, smeared with bruises
and the beach tar and twigs of ritual,
the couple spoke through their wounds
and fear of death, mumbling an exchange
of pledges and a curse for the Bay.

The following day, the charcoaled pillars
and collapsed floor still hissing,
a pair of cranes landed, loonlike,
from the overcast, snow-flurried skies.
A runaway chill spreading south from the Sierras
had brought them, and the steaming ruins
made their haven from the cold.
They danced a curious rite of celebration,
blue and grey-tipped wings furling,
red dandelion crests erect,
lifting from ground to air like curling smoke,
until, finally, be early evening,
they drifted downwind past the town

and landed cloudlike, small white floats,
plumed gardenias on the Rock's dark brow.

Love is always violent *and* sacred, and though death
might be peace, dying often seems love's own act,
a strong taking and the murder of reason.

All is true, a story sanded by several tellings
until it shines, jewel in the soft fingers of tide,
the constellated image high in its heaven of likenesses.

It doesn't matter how I think of it,
it continues to define itself,
this chunk of continent equal to nothing.

Fanny Howe

Born in 1940 in Buffalo, New York, Fanny Howe was educated at Stanford University. She has published many works of poetry and fiction, including *Forty Whacks, First Marriage, Bronte Wilde, The White Slave, Holy Smoke, In the Middle of Nowhere, The Lives of a Spirit*, and *Robeson Street*. Having taught literature at Emerson College and at Columbia and Tufts universities, Howe presently teaches in the writing program at the Massachusetts Institute of Technology. She lives in Boston with her three children.

Franklin Park

When snow falls on Franklin Park
and black grackles—

North, South, Central—sit between
each invisible spot of
happiness—the mothers walk by, brutally

into the old autumn gush of rust
red leaves

like you should be lucky to grow old
at all. I still see them, more of us.

Puddingstone, rutty and tough, in snow under their feet
turns into a soft thing thrown down

over the edge of dried myrtle and beech
leaves. Cars whir and curse

in front of what used to be our house
before our fortunes were reversed.

This America is a wonderful place,
one immigrant said. If it's a cage, then it's safe.

Down Robeson Street, away
from the park and zoo

    bends become
  calamities of bricked-up
  capital: those who
doze, mid-afternoon, meditate

bright close to time's receding

    glance and out.
    There's drink on the shelf,
grain in the pantry so the Padre

says it's not poverty we're getting used to

Refrigerators hum like animals
    running to music. A cutting
    wind rattles
out numbers, and minds organize
  each margin's going . . .

but it's just, he said, we got used to being.

Sprung out of sticks, fourteen lilacs
  hung over my fence from the tenement
next door.

Once, when pregnant,
and all for freedom,
I shook the rain off the wet, blue
flowers
and knew why it was that I was pregnant:
more lips to love more lilacs with.

In Franklin Park a daughter
held onto the swing

while a ward of the State,
a boy in frayed pants and shirt

for wiping dirt, his hair
snipped short, as if it were war,

watched me push, her pump.
Thin and whiter than most children,

he was motherless. Suddenly
she jumped into the red

leaves falling, her wild will
access to emergency.

My rage—always on call—
she never guessed was love,

she tells me now,
though I saw *he* knew.

As a guard in a baggy suit
is to a prisoner of politics,

so is wandering this park
to the eyes of a face like his,

wretched with exile's knowledge

and given—Pretorian—
to large shoes, a spare shirt.

Gone is the brush of dustball
curls, miniature clothes,

and vanished is the Cape of Good Hope.
Is somebody's son, yet.

Home to him's now a sandpaper map
of his mother's playground
credo: *expect nothing*

and put everything in its place.
Freedom's behind your face.

Pushing children in plaid & silver prams
us mothers were dumpy,
                    hunched in the damp

and our redlipped infants
     sucked on their strange fingers
          eyes stunned by the gunny-strong
               grass on near hills.

I wanted to sit near sweet water, or salt
in the fuzz of extreme weather,
          but we're not here to.

Like women who love the Lord live on hills

what for, what for, we cawed outside
          as in bare trees, too plain to see.

The snowflakes whirled, miniscule,
and three storey tenements
seemed to eat what was due

to the children in windows: pink lips
open on glass and frost . . . No sky
upstairs, but a wall surrounding

walls and a woman . . . Like this

happiness learned to be lonely before it could be lost and No,
no opiate made so many people as poor as this but pure
desire. And to those few I must say *yes* to their wish, "Let my
experience make me famous or rich." Your emptiness will
    come too, follow you from home and everywhere

        the courage to suffer is missing.

Andrew Hudgins

A native of Montgomery, Alabama, Andrew Hudgins' first book, *Saints and Strangers* (1985), was selected as part of the Houghton Mifflin New Poetry Series. His poems have appeared in *Poetry*, *The Kenyon Review*, *The New Yorker*, and *The Hudson Review*. Hudgins was a fellow at the Bread Loaf Writers Conference and a Wallace Stegner Fellow at Stanford University, where he won the Academy of American Poets Prize. He currently teaches at the University of Cincinnati.

Sentimental Dangers

When out of work and fierce with self-pity
I'd walk until the fierceness left my feet
and I broke down. Then I'd start home,
where once I walked up to find my wife
pitching a stick across the parking lot
while an ugly dog sat and looked at her.
She'd found him near the office where she typed,
and fed him half her sandwich. He'd hung around
until she'd given in and brought him home.
But he loved me so much that when I went
to play with him, he'd roll onto his back
and piss until it splattered on his chest.
I'd sit outside all afternoon and talk
to him, to the hard knowledge in his face
that she'd leave me when I was well enough

to be left. I talked too much. She'd tell her friends,
He's out of work. He thinks he is that dog.
And she was right, I did. But we were poor,
living on frozen chicken pies and tea—
I knew I'd have to take him to the pound.
As I signed him away with my right hand
and wiped my left—which he would not stop licking—
against the unwashed leg of my blue jeans
I felt I was signing myself away.
An illusion, sure, but one that lasted months.
I thought of this today when I crossed the bridge
and the river smelled like a wet, unwanted dog.

David Ignatow

David Ignatow was born in 1914 in Brooklyn, New York, and spent most of his life in the metropolitan area. He was a businessman for many years but eventually switched to an academic career. As either poet-in-residence or teacher, he was associated with such institutions as Vassar and York Colleges, and Kansas, Kentucky, and Long Island universities. Ignatow edited *The Beloit Poetry Journal* for a decade and also served as poetry editor for *The Nation* and co-editor of *Chelsea*. His poetry has appeared in such magazines as *Poetry*, *The Atlantic Monthly*, *The New Yorker*, and *Commentary*. He has received the Shelley Memorial Award, the Bollingen Prize in poetry, and an award from the National Institute of Arts and Letters "for a lifetime of creative effort."

In Memoriam: For Sam

David, I too have lost a son
whom I visit from time to time
at the Home for the mentally ill
and the aged. His brow wrinkles
with anxiety when I speak to him
in praise of his past. He is afraid
I am trying to push on him
a character and ambition that are not
his. Yet he smiles when I arrive
as if that much he remembers
of the past, that I am his father,

that he must have been a child
to have had a father.

I no longer have a son, David.
I visit him as one visits periodically
the site of an unmitigated disaster
to renew one's memory of the once living
who lost their lives at that site.
It comforts me that at least
the past exists in his being, though
it no longer is in him and no longer
attests to his life. It is I
who keep his past alive in my thoughts.
They restore in me my belief
that life can be good. There once
was proof and the proof is
that he exists if but a monument
to that past. When I leave him
with his box of cookies I am
on my way to my own life
affirmed in its reality
by having visited with him.

Lawrence Joseph

Born in Detroit, Michigan in 1948, Lawrence Joseph was educated at the University of Michigan, where he received the Hopwood Award. He then attended the University of Michigan Law School. His first poetry collection, *Shouting At No One* (University of Pittsburgh: 1983), received the 1982 Starrett Poetry Prize. *Curriculum Vitae*, his second collection, will be published by the University of Pittsburgh Press in 1987. From 1982 to 1985, Joseph was an editor of the British international quarterly *Stand*. In 1984 he received a National Endowment for the Arts Poetry Award. A professor of law at Hofstra Law School, he has served as a judicial law clerk to the Chief Justice of the Michigan Supreme Court and has acted as a consultant to the Governor of Michigan on occupational disease compensation. He lives with his wife, the painter Nancy Van Goethem, in New York City.

Any and All

You draw nearer to see her more closely,
the blind woman by the bronze doors

of the old Merchants Bank, her mouth
wide open as if in a silent roar,

several dollars stuffed in the pockets
of her mink coat. She is easy to forget

a few days later when you think of her
—not long. The phone is ringing.

You put Byrdman on hold. Polen
wants you in his office immediately.

The lawyers from Mars and the bankers
from Switzerland have arrived to close the deal.

the money in their heads articulated
to the debt of the state of Bolivia.

How much later the Croatian woman
who empties the wastebaskets laughs

when you answer you've been better
and you've been worse. How much sooner

you're told not to tell anyone Byrdman's
grandfather was a Jew. How much No. 54

Wall Street, emblematic reality of extreme
speculations and final effects.

The other evening at a party in the West Sixties
you say as much. None of them knows

what any of it is worth, you say to yourself
later spitting into an unexpected breeze.

Yellow moons of street lamps on Ninth Avenue
obscured by atmospheric soot and fog,

in the Twenties empty windows of butcher shops,
factories and warehouses without names,

no taxis, the green light behind the window
of a corner bar. A young man sporting muscles,

a woman he might own on his arm, clearly
doesn't like the way you look or look at him,

lets his leash out enough for his wolfdog
to just nip your leg. Another day

you contemplate your strategy:
think about how they think about you

thinking about them and the look on your face
to prove you have the proper attitude.

Let no laughter reveal moods. Let
Charlotte Stone reveal that her father

over the weekend purchased a peninsula in Rhode Island
for Harry and her, let her teeth

be too large and too gray: there is blood
and there is blood-letting; this is not your blood.

Shut the door and wait. Someone else's father
forgives you when you know not what you do,

reminds you, "He's a weasel but he's my friend."
You're a monkey and you work for him,

decide for him whether his clauses should be restrictive,
whether to replace every "any" with "all."

X.J. Kennedy

Born in 1929, Joseph Charles Kennedy is a native of Dover, New Jersey. He studied at both Seton Hall College and Columbia University before serving four years in the U.S. Navy. He later continued his education at the Sorbonne. He has taught at various universities and, from 1926 until 1964, was the editor of *The Paris Review*. His first collection, *Nude Descending a Staircase*, won the Lamont Poetry Award for 1961; he is one of the few poets who continues to write in traditional meters and rhymes. A National Endowment for the Arts Grant, a Shelley Memorial Award, and a Guggenheim Fellowship are among his achievements. His most recent book is *Cross Ties* (University of Georgia Press: 1985), and he is currently living with his wife in Massachusetts.

Cross Ties

Out walking ties left over from a track
Where nothing travels now but rust and grass,
I could take stock in something that would pass
Bearing down Hell-bent from behind my back:
A thing to sidestep or go down before,
Far-off, indifferent as that curfew's wail
The evening wind flings like a sack of mail
Or close up as the moon whose headbeam stirs
A flock of cloud to make tracks. Down to strafe
Bristle-backed grass a hawk falls—there's a screech
Like steel wrenched taut till severed. Out of reach

Or else beneath desiring, I go safe,
Walk on, tensed for a leap, unreconciled
To a dark void all kindness.
                        When I spill
The salt I throw the Devil some and, still,
I let them sprinkle water on my child.

Jane Kenyon

Born in Ann Arbor, Michigan in 1947, Jane Kenyon received a B.A. in 1970 and an M.A. in 1972 from the University of Michigan. For five years she co-edited the literary magazine *Green House*, which she also co-founded. She has written two books of poetry, *From Room to Room* (Alice James: 1978) and *The Boat of Quiet Hours* (Graywolf: 1986), and has translated *Twenty Poems of Anna Akhmatova*. Her work appears in such magazines as *The Paris Review*, *The New Yorker*, *The Iowa Review*, and *New Letters*. Kenyon has read at many colleges and universities and has also performed on radio. Her honors include the Avery Hopwood Award and fellowships from the National Endowment for the Arts and the New Hampshire Commission on the Arts.

Trouble with Math in a One-Room Country School

The others bent their heads and started in.
Confused, I asked my neighbor
to explain—a sturdy, bright-cheeked girl
who brought raw milk to school from her family's
herd of Holsteins. Ann had a blue bookmark,
and on it Christ revealed his beating heart,
holding the flesh back with his wounded hand.
Ann understood division. . . .

Miss Moran sprang from her monumental desk
and led me roughly through the class

without a word. My shame was radical
as she propelled me past the cloakroom
to the furnace closet, where only the boys
were put, only the older ones at that.
The door swung briskly shut.

The warmth, the gloom, the smell
of sweeping compound clinging to the broom
soothed me. I found a bucket, turned it
upside down, and sat, hugging my knees.
I hummed a theme from Haydn that I knew
from my piano lessons . . .
and hardened my heart against authority.
And then I heard her steps, her fingers
on the latch. She led me, blinking
and changed, back to the class.

Faye Kicknosway

Who Shall Know Them? (Viking: 1985) is Faye Kicknosway's first poetry collection published by a large press. Six volumes, many of which she had also illustrated, were published by small presses. Known for her artwork as well as her poetry, Kicknosway's drawings have been included in many juried and invitational shows. She is a recent recipient of a National Endowment for the Arts Fellowship and currently lives in Bloomsfield, Michigan.

I Don't Know Her

This woman here, sloppy-shouldered,
squint-eyed, I don't know her.
Nor this room
she's in. Those wooden walls
and floors. All stained-up.
All whopper-jawed
and needing nails and paint.
I don't know her.

The size
of her nose or her mouth
pulled up. The sleeping kid
she holds.
I couldn't name you her

if you asked me. Nor him,
nor the rest of them all lined out
and held so still. Unnatural.
I've seen fish
on a string
down a country boy's back
look more natural
than they look, posed close
together, not scratching, not
with the window opened and the old
one there, looking out.

And his handkerchief's not knotted
tight
on his neck like he usually wears it.

And her, with the safety pin,
the young
one, getting long-boned and moony,
scratching her toes
against the wood, I don't know her,
neither.
Nor do I care to.
That suspicious old lady,
head cocked, sideways looking out
at me, new shoelaces in her shoes,
I wouldn't look out
my window
to look at her, nor listen
to her talking
at the vegetables
in her backyard garden.

None of them is worth the time
and they've all
been dead

longer years than I been born
and living.
And the road out front
don't lead no where near their house, it
sitting in the hollow
down lower than that stand
of trees out back
of the chicken coop.

And that little picture tacked
on the wall back there

where the old man can see it
but the kids have to stand
on the wash tub turned over,
don't mean a thing to me.

And the shirt
over the door, you can see its
collar here, I've never seen it
on anyone
or anyplace other than right
there, it's always been just like that,
partly visible, at the top
of the picture.

But mostly her,
it's mostly her
I don't know. I maybe seen
pictures of rooms
like this, and kids
sleeping or awake—all tilt-faced
and dreamy-eyed
like that one, or wanting to run
by the side
of the house with the dog,

throwing sticks
and giggling, like that little one
there
held in between his father's knees—
I maybe seen

kids like that, running in the street
or in the alley.

Even that old lady, I've seen her
too, or someone like her,
peeking around a curtain, the room
behind her
dark and never opened. And him,

he's everywhere; I see him
any time of the day.
But her,
I've never seen her.
That big hand rolled into a fist,
those feet bent double
under her,
that little edge of slip
showing underneath her checker dress; no,

I've never seen her before
nor do I care to see her now.
Her hair
all knotted
and black, those bug bites

showing on her chest
where her dress is opened.
The dirt on her and how she's all
slopped down
on the edge of the bed looking like

she hasn't any sense at all
behind her face.
I don't know her nor
do I care to.

She leaves that baby whining
on the floor
while she goes off in the field
looking for men.
She leaves it between chairs
so it can't crawl too far.
Everyday
she leaves it. She goes farther
and farther, sometimes

disappears in the weeds,
sometimes stands in the shade
of the trees looking out
at the men and rubbing her hand
on her arm
or scratching at the ticks
on her legs. She squints

under her hand and sometimes follows
the road, wagons coming along,

sometimes cars. She lies herself down
under a tree

and everything stalls
right there.
She's slower and slower
getting back. One day you'll take this

picture out to show me, to have me
story it for you, and there'll be

an empty place at the corner
of the bed. And the baby

will be all knotted up
and asleep on the sheet
with no momma anywhere near it.
She'll be gone,
she'll have disappeared down the road
so far
there'll be no time to call her back
so you can show me this

picture with her in it.
She'll be in the shade
of a tree or in the shade
of some man's arms.
And none of them
will see it, they'll all

be right there, lined up, looking straight
ahead and never sideways to see
if she's made it back in time.
She'll be gone,

and nobody will notice. The bed
will be ditched in from having
her weight on it in that spot
for so long, and the baby
will be asleep.
Nobody will notice.

You'll show me this picture
and I'll say, "Look at how

funny that bed looks, like someone's
been sitting on it."

And there won't be any way for me
to tell you about her;
she'll be gone.

And I could meet her on the street
and she could hello me
until her throat
got dusty, I wouldn't hear her.
You got to know
someone before you can hear them.
Before you can answer back.
And I don't know her.

Galway Kinnell

Galway Kinnell was born in 1927 in Providence, Rhode Island, and was educated at Princeton University. Since 1955, when he studied in Paris on a Fulbright Scholarship, he has travelled and lived in Europe, Iran, and throughout the United States. While living in the southern United States, he became active in the Civil Rights Movement, and in 1963 he was a field worker for the Congress of Racial Equality. Kinnell has been the recipient of numerous honors including a Rockefeller Grant (1967), a Guggenheim Fellowship (1974), and the Pulitzer Prize for poetry in 1982. *First Poems 1946–1954* and *The Avenue Bearing the Initial of Christ into the New World: Poems 1946–1964* collect his earlier work. His latest work is *The Past* (Houghton Mifflin: 1985).

The Road Between Here and There

Here I heard the terrible chaste snorting of hogs trying to re-enter
   the underearth.
Here I came into the curve too fast, on ice, and being new to
   these winters, touched the brake and sailed into the pasture.
Here I stopped the car and snoozed while two small children
   crawled all over me.
Here I reread *Moby Dick* (skimming big chunks, even though to
   me it is the greatest of all novels) in a single day, while Fergus
   fished.
Here I abandoned the car because of a clonk in the motor and

hitchhiked (which in those days in Vermont meant walking
the whole way with a limp) all the way to a garage where I
passed the afternoon with ex-loggers who had stopped by to
oil the joints of their artificial limbs.
Here a barn burned down to the snow. "Friction," one of the ex-
loggers said. "Friction?" "Yup, the mortgage, rubbing against
the insurance policy."
Here I went eighty but was in no danger of arrest, for I was
"blessed speeding"—trying to get home in time to see my
children before they slept.
Here I bought speckled brown eggs with bits of straw shitted to
them.
Here I brought home in the back seat two piglets who rummaged
inside the burlap sack like pregnancy itself.
Here I heard on the car radio Handel's concerto for harp and lute
for the second time in my life, which Inés played to me the
first time, making me want to drive after it and hear it forever.
Here I hurt with mortal thoughts and almost recovered.
Here I sat on a boulder by the winter-steaming river and put my
head in my hands and considered time—which is next to
nothing, merely what vanishes, and yet can make one's elbows
nearly pierce one's thighs.
Here I forgot how to sing in the old way and listened to frogs at
dusk make their more angelic croaking.
Here the local fortune teller took my hand and said, "What is
still possible is inspired work, faithfulness to a few, and a last
love, which, being last, will be like looking up and seeing the
parachute dissolving in a shower of gold."
Here is the chimney standing up by itself and falling down,
which tells you you approach the end of the road between here
and there.
Here I arrive there.
Here I must turn around and go back and on the way back look

carefully to left and to right.

For here, the moment all the spaces along the road between here
and there—which the young know are infinite and all others
know are not—get used up, that's it.

John Knoepfle

Born in Cincinnati, Ohio in 1923, John Knoepfle received his M.A. from Xavier University in 1951. Before entering college, he served four years in the Navy during World War II and was awarded a Purple Heart. In 1967 he earned a Ph.D. from St. Louis University. Knoepfle has taught school, worked for an educational television station as a producer and director, and has been a government consultant. He has translated the poetry of Cesar Vallego and Wang Shouyi and has published more than ten books of original poetry, most recently *Poems from the Sangamon* (University of Illinois Press, 1985). His honors include a National Endowment for the Arts Grant and a Guggenheim Fellowship. Knoepfle is currently a professor of literature at Sangamon State University in Springfield, Illinois.

east in mclean county

this is a country of moraines
old prairie could have
gone on forever

mounds timbers points
groves islands savannas
a language of prairies

farmhouses on the high places
barns outbuildings
washed in the clear air

corn fields and soybean
enough for everyone

east of ellsworth
an osage orange hedge
stiffens the curve of the earth

four crows carry the sky away cawing

Kenneth Koch

Kenneth Koch was born in 1925 and was raised in Cincinnati, Ohio. During World War II he served in the United States Army as a rifleman and was stationed in the Pacific. After the war, he received a B.A. from Harvard University, where he met John Ashbery and Frank O'Hara. He obtained a doctorate from Columbia University in 1959. Koch spent three years living in Europe and during that time was influenced by contemporary French poetry. He has published more than a dozen books of verse and is a playwright whose dramatic works, from 1951 to 1971, can be found in the anthology *A Change of Hearts*. Koch's honors include two Fulbright Fellowships in 1950 and 1978, a Guggenheim Fellowship in 1961, a National Endowment for the Arts Grant in 1966, and a National Institute of Arts and Letters Award in 1976. His books on the teaching of poetry to young children and the elderly have been highly acclaimed. He currently lives in New York, where he is a professor of English at Columbia University.

The Circus

I remember when I wrote The Circus
I was living in Paris, or rather we were living in Paris
Janice, Frank was alive, the Whitney Museum
Was still on 8th Street, or was it still something else?
Fernand Léger lived in our building
Well it wasn't really our building it was the building we
    lived in

Next to a Grand Guignol troupe who made a lot of
    noise
So that one day I yelled through a hole in the wall
Of our apartment I don't know why there was a hole
    there
Shut up! And the voice came back to me saying
    something
I don't know what. Once I saw Léger walk out of the
    building
I think. Stanley Kunitz came to dinner. I wrote The
    Circus
In two tries, the first getting most of the first stanza;
That fall I also wrote an opera libretto called Louisa or
    Matilda.
Jean-Claude came to dinner. He said (about ''cocktail
    sauce'')
It should be good on something but not on these
    (oysters).
By that time I think I had already written The Circus.
Part of the inspiration came while walking to the post
    office one night
And I wrote a big segment of The Circus
When I came back, having been annoyed to have to go
I forget what I went there about
You were back in the apartment what a dump actually
    we liked it
I think with your hair and your writing and the pans
Moving strummingly about the kitchen and I wrote
    The Circus
It was a summer night no it was an autumn one summer
    when
I remember it but actually no autumn that black dusk
    toward the post office
And I wrote many other poems then but The Circus
    was the best
Maybe not by far the best Geography was also wonder-

ful
And the Airplane Betty poems (inspired by you) but
    The Circus was the best.
Sometimes I feel I actually am the person
Who did this, who wrote that, including that poem The
    Circus
But sometimes on the other hand I don't.
There are so many factors engaging our attention!
At every moment the happiness of others, the health of
    those we know and our own!
And the millions upon millions of people we don't
    know and their well-being to think about
So it seems strange I found time to write The Circus
And even spent two evenings on it, and that I have also
    the time
To remember that I did it, and remember you and me
    then, and write this poem about it
At the beginning of The Circus
The Circus girls are rushing through the night
In the circus wagons and tulips and other flowers will be
    picked
A long time from now this poem wants to get off on its
    own
Someplace like a painting not held to a depiction of
    composing The Circus.

Noel Lee was in Paris then but usually out of it
In Germany or Denmark giving a concert
As part of an endless activity
Which was either his career or his happiness or a
    combination of both
Or neither I remember his dark eyes looking he was
    nervous
With me perhaps because of our days at Harvard.

It is understandable enough to be nervous with any-
    body!

How softly and easily one feels when alone
Love of one's friends when one is commanding the time
    and space syndrome
If that's the right word which I doubt but together how
    come one is so nervous?
One is not always but what was I then and what am I
    now attempting to create
If create is the right word
Out of this combination of experience and aloneness
And who are you telling me it is or is not a poem (not
    you)? Go back with me though
To those nights I was writing The Circus.
Do you like that poem? have you read it? It is in my
    book Thank You
Which Grove just reprinted. I wonder how long I am
    going to live
And what the rest will be like I mean the rest of my life.

John Cage said to me the other night How old are you?
    and I told him forty-six
(Since then I've become forty-seven) he said
Oh that's a great age I remember.
John Cage once told me he didn't charge much for his
    mushroom identification course (at the New
    School)
Because he didn't want to make a profit from nature

He was ahead of his time I was behind my time we were
    both in time
Brilliant go to the head of the class and "time is a river"
It doesn't seem like a river to me it seems like an
    unformed plan
Days go by and still nothing is decided about

What to do until you know it never will be and then
    you say "time"
But you really don't care much about it any more
Time means something when you have the major part
    of yours ahead of you
As I did in Aix-en-Provence that was three years before I
    wrote The Circus
That year I wrote Bricks and The Great Atlantic
    Rainway
I felt time surround me like a blanket endless and soft
I could go to sleep endlessly and wake up and still be in
    it
But I treasured secretly the part of me that was
    individually changing
Like Noel Lee I was interested in my career
And still am but now it is like a town I don't want to
    leave
Not a tower I am climbing opposed by ferocious
    enemies

I never mentioned my friends in my poems at the time I
    wrote The Circus
Although they meant almost more than anything to me
Of this now for some time I've felt an attenuation
So I'm mentioning them maybe this will bring them
    back to me
Not them perhaps but what I felt about them
John Ashbery Jane Freilicher Larry Rivers Frank
    O'Hara
Their names alone bring tears to my eyes
As seeing Polly did last night

It is beautiful at any time but the paradox is leaving it
In order to feel it when you've come back the sun has
    declined

And the people are merrier or else they've gone home
    altogether
And you are left alone well you put up with that your
    sureness is like the sun
While you have it but when you don't its lack's a black
    and icy night. I came home

And wrote The Circus that night, Janice. I didn't come
    and speak to you
And put my arm around you and ask you if you'd like to
    take a walk
Or go to the Cirque Medrano though that's what I
    wrote poems about
And am writing about that now, and now I'm alone

And this is not as good a poem as The Circus
And I wonder if any good will come of either of them
    all the same.

Edgar Koerner

Born in Vienna, Austria in 1932, Edgar Koerner received a B.A. and an M.A. from Harvard University. His poems have appeared in various literary magazines and have been read over National Public Radio. When not writing poetry, he is president of a music school and advisory director of an investment bank. He lives in New York City with his wife.

Grandfather Ernst at Ebbets Field

He had the only dark three-piece suit
in the packed upper deck high over home plate
that sweltering night he had decided
we'd do something together now I was twelve,
whatever I wanted, but no girlie shows.
On the subway to Brooklyn he told me it would be
the first sport he'd gone to since Salzburg beat Graz
in the Football Cup Final of '37
at the old South Vienna Football Park
(creamed by our bombers seven years later).
I pictured those stands full of old men
in dark three-piece suits, their hats in their laps,
sitting just as he sat that hot night in Brooklyn,
politely bewildered, pretending his interest.

Why doesn't he run? You can't on a foul.
Who decided nine innings? That's just how it is.
You did your homework? I told you I did.

And then the ball that came slowly rising,
foul, high above us in a towering arc:
at its highest, it seemed to stop,
scan the crowd, and then slowly home
toward section thirteen, where he was the only one
still in his seat. He held up his hand,
but he didn't catch it, it just settled in.

I saw those old men in the stands in Vienna
again that same night, just before sleep.
They smiled, waved their hats, and wished me good night.

Maxine Kumin

Born in 1925 and raised in Germantown, Philadelphia, Maxine
Kumin received a B.A. and an M.A. from Radcliffe College. She
has taught at such universities as Columbia, Brandeis, and Princeton.
In 1973, *Up Country* was awarded the Pulitzer Prize for poetry.
Kumin has written over twenty children's books, of these three were
collaborations with her friend, the late poet Anne Sexton. For the
year 1981–1982 she was Consultant in Poetry at the Library of
Congress. Of her seven volumes of poetry the most recent is *The
Long Approach* (Viking: 1985). She currently lives in Warner, New
Hampshire.

Getting Through

I want to apologize
for all the snow falling in
this poem so early in the season.
Falling on the calendar of bad news.
Already we have had snow lucid,
snow surprising, snow bees
and lambswool snow. Already
snows of exaltation have covered
some scars. Larks and the likes
of paisleys went up. But lately the sky
is letting down large-print flakes
of old age. Loving this poor place,
wanting to stay on, we have endured

134

an elegiac snow of whitest jade,
subdued biographical snows
and public storms, official and profuse.

Even if the world is ending
you can tell it's February
by the architecture of the pastures.
Snow falls on the pregnant mares,
is followed by a thaw, and then
refreezes so that everywhere
their hill upheaves into a glass mountain.
The horses skid, stiff-legged, correct
position, break through the crust
and stand around disconsolate
lipping wisps of hay.
Animals are said to be soulless.
Unable to anticipate.

No mail today.
No newspapers. The phone's dead.
Bombs and grenades, the newly disappeared,
a kidnapped ear, go unrecorded
but the foals flutter inside
warm wet bags that carry them
eleven months in the dark.
It seems they lie transversely, thick
as logs. The outcome is well known.
If there's an April
in the last frail snow of April
they will knock hard to be born.

Stanley Kunitz

Born in Worcester, Massachusetts in 1905, Stanley Kunitz graduated *summa cum laude* from Harvard University. *Intellectual Things* (Doubleday: 1930), his first book of poems, was followed by several others, including the Pulitzer Prize winner *Selected Poems 1928– 1958*. His latest book is *Next-to-Last Things: New Poems and Essays* (1985). In addition to this original poetry, he has translated the Russian poets Anna Akhmatova, Yevgeny Yevtushenko, and Andrei Voznesensky. Since 1928 Kunitz has edited reference books, including eight major dictionaries of literary biographies, and he is an authority on European, British, and American literatures. He was a Consultant in Poetry at the Library of Congress in Washington, D.C., and from 1969 to 1976 he was editor of the Yale Series of Younger Poets. He has also published criticism and has taught writing and literature internationally. Kunitz's many honors include a Guggenheim Fellowship, a Ford Grant, the Brandeis Medal of Achievement, and several honorary degrees. A senior fellow at the National Endowment for the Arts and a member of the American Academy of Arts and Letters, Kunitz was elected a chancellor of the Academy of American Poets in 1970. He currently lives in New York City and Provincetown, Massachusetts, with his wife, the painter Elise Asher.

The Wellfleet Whale

A few summers ago, on Cape Cod, a whale foundered on the beach, a sixty-three-foot finback whale. When the tide went out, I

approached him. He was lying there, in monstrous desolation,
making the most terrifying noises—rumbling—groaning. I put my
hands on his flanks and I could feel the life inside him. And while
I was standing there, suddenly he opened his eye. It was a big,
red, cold eye, and it was staring directly at me. A shudder of
recognition passed between us. Then the eye closed forever. I've
been thinking about whales ever since.

—Journal entry

1

You have your language too,
   an eerie medley of clicks
     and hoots and trills,
location-notes and love calls,
   whistles and grunts. Occasionally,
     it's like furniture being smashed,
or the creaking of a mossy door,
   sounds that all melt into a liquid
     song with endless variations,
as if to compensate
   for the vast loneliness of the sea.
     Sometimes a disembodied voice
breaks in, as if from distant reefs,
   and it's as much as one can bear
     to listen to its long mournful cry,
a sorrow without name, both more
   and less than human. It drags
     across the ear like a record
running down.

2

No wind. No waves. No clouds.
   Only the whisper of the tide,
     as it withdrew, stroking the shore,

a lazy drift of gulls overhead,
　　and tiny points of light
　　　　bubbling in the channel.
It was the tag-end of summer.
　　From the harbor's mouth
　　　　you coasted into sight,
flashing news of your advent,
　　the crescent of your dorsal fin
　　　　clipping the diamonded surface.
We cheered at the sign of your greatness
　　when the black barrel of your head
　　　　erupted, ramming the water,
and you flowered for us
　　in the jet of your spouting.

　　　　　　　　3
All afternoon you swam
　　tirelessly round the bay,
　　　　with such an easy motion,
the slightest downbeat of your tail,
　　an almost imperceptible
　　　　undulation of your flippers,
you seemed like something poured,
　　not driven; you seemed
　　　　to marry grace with power.
And when you bounded into air,
　　slapping your flukes,
　　　　we thrilled to look upon
pure energy incarnate
　　as nobility of form.
　　　　You seemed to ask of us
not sympathy, or love,
　　or understanding,
　　　　but awe and wonder.

That night we watched you
　　swimming in the moon.
　　　Your back was molten silver.
We guessed your silent passage
　　by the phosphorescence in your wake.
　　　At dawn we found you stranded on the rocks.

4

There came a boy and a man
　　and yet other men running, and two
　　　schoolgirls in yellow halters
and a housewife bedecked
　　with curlers, and whole families in beach
　　　buggies with assorted yelping dogs.
The tide was almost out.
　　We could walk around you,
　　　as you heaved deeper into the shoal,
crushed by your own weight,
　　collapsing into yourself,
　　　your flippers and your flukes
quivering, your blowhole
　　spasmodically bubbling, roaring.
　　　In the pit of your gaping mouth
you bared your fringework of baleen,
　　a thicket of horned bristles.
　　　When the Curator of Mammals
arrived from Boston
　　to take samples of your blood
　　　you were alrcady oozing from below.
Somebody had carved his initials
　　in your flank. Hunters of souvenirs
　　　had peeled off strips of your skin,
a membrane thin as paper.
　　You were blistered and cracked by the sun.
　　　The gulls had been pecking at you.
The sound you made was a hoarse and fitful bleating.

What drew us, like a magnet, to your dying?
    You made a bond between us,
        the keepers of the nightfall watch,
who gathered in a ring around you,
    boozing in the bonfire light.
Toward dawn we shared with you
your hour of desolation,
    the huge lingering passion
        of your unearthly outcry,
as you swung your blind head
    toward us and laboriously opened
        a bloodshot, glistening eye,
in which we swam with terror and recognition.

                    5
Voyager, chief of the pelagic world,
    you brought with you the myth
        of another country, dimly remembered,
where flying reptiles
    lumbered over the steaming marshes
        and trumpeting thunder lizards
wallowed in the reeds.
    While empires rose and fell on land,
        your nation breasted the open main,
rocked in the consoling rhythm
    of the tides. Which ancestor first plunged
        head-down through zones of colored twilight
to scour the bottom of the dark?
    You ranged the North Atlantic track
        from Port-of-Spain to Baffin Bay,
edging between the ice-floes
    through the fat of summer,
        lob-tailing, breaching, sounding,
grazing in the pastures of the sea
    on krill-rich orange plankton
        crackling with life.

You prowled down the continental shelf,
  guided by the sun and stars
   and the taste of alluvial silt
on your way southward
  to the warm lagoons,
   the tropic of desire,
where the lovers lie belly to belly
  in the rub and nuzzle of their sporting;
   and you turned, like a god in exile,
out of your wide primeval element,
  delivered to the mercy of time.
   Master of the whale-roads,
let the white wings of the gulls
  spread out their cover.
   You have become like us,
disgraced and mortal.

Richmond Lattimore

Born in Paotingfou, China, Richmond Lattimore came to the United States at the age of fourteen. He was educated at Dartmouth College and at the University of Illinois, where he received a Ph.D. Lattimore is a renowned translator of classical literature whose publications include two collections of Pindaric odes, Aeschylus' *Oresteia* (1953), the *Illiad* (1951), and the *Odyssey* (1967). He taught Greek at Bryn Mawr from 1935 to 1971 and was a senior fellow at the Center for Hellenic Studies in Washington, D.C., from 1960 to 1965. Beginning with *Poems* (1957), Lattimore's original poetry collections include *Poems from Three Decades* (1972) and *Continuing Conclusions* (1983). His honors include a ten thousand dollar Annual Fellowship Award from the Academy of American Poets. Lattimore died in 1984 at the age of seventy-seven.

The Idea of a Town

There had to be a water-tower in a grove on the highest
point, and at the flattest the railroad yards and the stations;
at least one street a hundred feet wide running

through the entire town, to the ghost edges laid out
in blocks with nothing there but the sidewalks and hydrants.
The schools, unravished still by the moderns; the little

playground with its swings. The modest cluster
of stores and offices desperately down town. The movie house.
A handful of little apartment buildings. Beyond them, acre

on acre, on the straight streets (Race, Main, Front, Poplar),
the houses of the people, two story, with tiny
lawns, and swings on the porches. Remember? This was
    America's

unimaginative matrix of all our imagination and dreamstuff.

James Laughlin

Born in 1914 in Pittsburgh, Pennsylvania, James Laughlin received
an A.B. from Harvard University in 1939. As founder and president
of New Directions Publishing Corporation, Laughlin edited twenty-
eight volumes of *New Directions in Prose and Poetry* between the
years 1937 and 1974. He has also written several volumes of poetry.
Laughlin's honors include a P.E.N. Publishers Citation and an
American Academy of Arts and Letters Distinguished Service
Award. He is a member of the American Academy of Arts and
Sciences.

The Deconstructed Man

Multas per gentes et multa per aequora vectus
(et multas per vias quoque aereas)
(there being no flugbuggies in the time of
    Gaius Valerius)
through many lands by shores of many peoples
a life too short sometimes
at times a life too long-seeming
the days of sun and rain and many days of
    mountain snow
the nights of endless dreaming
my periplum more geographically extended
(in Java the airplane is the god Garuda)
but I learned less not being polumetis

and my paideuma is a mishmash of contradictions
my Circes a list of fictions

Muse help me to sing
of Toodles on the wide beach of Troorak
(her hair so golden and her brain so slack)
of darling Leontina di Rapallo
taking me to her underwater cave
(J'ai rêvé dans la grotte où nage la sirène
I have lingered in the chambers of the sea)
of Dylan's crazy Daphne in the Gargoyle Club
   in Soho
(Voi che sapete che cosa è amor . . .
Sento un affeto pien di desir
ch'ora è diletto ch'ora è martir)
of delicate moonlit Delia by the Strait of
   Juan DeFuca
of Cynthia whom I helped the gods destroy
in ogne parte dove mi trae memoria
of name-is-gone-but-not-her-smile
there in the jungle near Chichen Itza
(A ristorar le pene d'un innocente amor)
of Kyo-San (they had girl caddies on the course at
   Kamakura)
(Ma in Ispagna son già mille e tre)
a list of fictions of beautiful contradictions
Lord Krishna's lotus and Williams' asphodel
each one so wonderful so new bringing her
   particular magic
risplende ognun sa luce che non morirà mai
and Restif said there were a thousand women who
   were always one
sola et magna (mater)
Gertrude's Mother of us All
I penetrate thy temple and thou doest my soul
   restore

ineffable thou art the Virgin & the Whore
I lusted for Tom's Wendy in Kentucky there was
   guilt
his sin (if it were sin for him) but surely mine
a list of fictions of contradictions
ma basta per oggi il catalogo delle fanciulle
who cares though I cared everywhere and always
the sea was not my mother but my mother took me
   to the sea
the old Cunarder Mauretania and Bill the sailor
who showed me how to splice a rope
and Jack turned green when we were beating
   through the chop above Grenada
avoid the Indian Ocean you can die of heat
posh P & O boats are like baking ovens
the sea the sea cried Xenophon after his weary
   march
O mother sea our bodies turn to dust our hearts
   return to thee
but it's the air we breathe and now in the air we fly
what would the many-crafted Odysseus make of
   that
he never saw as I have seen from the cabin window
   of the plane
glistening Mont Blanc and holy Kanchenjunga and
   mystic Fuji
by Isfahan he never saw those traceries
of ancient water tunnels on the desert below
he did not see the million lights of cities in the night
cities now doomed to die
these things he never saw
but what he saw and did will live as long as we

I am the deconstructed man
my parts are scattered on the nursery floor
and can't be put back together again because

the instruction book is lost
clean up your mess in the nursery my mother says
I am the deconstructed man
my older brother laughs at me all the time
he drives me into a rage and I drive the scissors
     into his knee
he has to have six stitches at the hospital and go
     on crutches but I pay for my jubilation
look mother James is doing it again he's chewing
     with his mouth open
and he hasn't learned his lines of catechism for
     Sunday
God went back to Heaven when I was twelve
     He stopped counting the hairs of my head
will he ever come back? I was waiting for Him
     then but now I'm waiting for Godot
Pound said "C'est moi dans la poubelle."
they had to chop us both up to get us into that
     trashcan in Paris
but why was there no blood? there's never any
     blood
did Abel bleed? did En Bertrans the sower of
     discord bleed
there in the bolge holding his severed head by the
     hair and swinging it like a lantern
E'l capo tronco tenea per la chiome
Pesol con mano a guisa di lanterna
E quel mirava noi, e dicea "oh me!!"
(Bos chavaliers fo e bos guerriers . . .
e bos trobaire e savis e be parlans . . .)
why don't I bleed what is it that my heart is
     pumping?
Cynthia said it was embalming fluid and she went
     away
like God and mother Cynthia went away

I am the deconstructed man
I do the best I can

Lie quiet Ezra there in your campo santo on San
   Michele
in paradisum deducant te angeli
to your city of Dioce to Wagadu to your paradiso
   terrestre
what I have reft from you I stole for love of you
belovéd my master and my friend.

David Lehman

Born in 1948 in New York City, David Lehman studied at Columbia and Cambridge universities and received his Ph.D. in 1978. He has taught at Brooklyn College, Hamilton College, and Cornell University, and he is currently a professor of English at Columbia University. The founding editor of Nobadaddy Press, Lehman was poetry editor for the *New York Arts Journal* from 1976 to 1980. He has published criticism and poetry, including his latest poetry collection *Alternative to Speech* (Princeton University Press). He frequently contributes poems and reviews to *Poetry*, *The Paris Review*, *The Partisan Review*, *Newsday*, and the *Times Literary Supplement*.

Arbeit Macht Frei

"Work shall set you free:" a sensible sentiment:
Marx would agree: Freud would give his assent:

Yet take those words and put them on a sign
And hang that sign upon the gate at Auschwitz,

What happens then: it means "abandon hope all ye who
    enter here:"
And that is exactly the relation between language and
    truth,

Said the professor: yes, and if life is but a dream
Of paradise, it's a nightmare with a happy ending:

Waking, we forget we were thieves of Eden in our sleep:
The others who slept in our room last night are gone,

But we go on, aping their gestures of resigned
Acceptance, knowing we shouldn't envy

The heroes of the late nineteenth century
Whose crucial fictions can mean nothing to us today,

Yet envy them we do, while in the deserted classroom,
Obscured from view, the unerased blackboard awaits

The eraser monitor's fresh wet sponge:
Quick, write down the formula, pretending that it's true:

Don't ask why: this is nervous bliss, this refusal to take
Pain to the piano with you, this quiet cry.

Denise Levertov

Born in 1923 in Essex, England, Denise Levertov was educated at home by her parents. She arrived in the United States at the age of twenty-five, after serving as a nurse in London during the Second World War. In 1947 she married an American novelist, Mitchell Goodman, and was naturalized in 1955. Levertov has taught at many colleges and universities, including the University of California at Berkeley and the Massachusetts Institute of Technology. In 1961 she was poetry editor of *The Nation*. Over thirty of her works have been published; *Breathing the Water* is forthcoming from New Directions. Her many honors include a Guggenheim Fellowship and an election to the National Institute of Arts and Letters. She currently lives in Somerville, Massachusetts.

During a Son's Dangerous Illness

You could die before me—
I've known it
always, the
dreaded worst, 'unnatural' but
possible
in the play
of matter, matter and
growth and
fate.

        *

My sister Philippa died
twelve years before I was born—
the perfect, laughing firstborn,
a gift to be cherished as my orphaned mother
had not been cherished. Suddenly:
death, a baby

cold and still.
                    *
Parent, child—death ignores
protocol, a sweep of its cape brushes
this one or that one at random
into the dust, it was
not even looking.
                    What becomes
of the past if the future
snaps off, brittle,
the present left as a jagged edge
opening on nothing?
                    *
Grief for the menaced world—lost rivers,
poisoned lakes—all creatures, perhaps,
to be fireblasted
                    off the
whirling cinder we
loved, but not enough . . .
The grief I'd know if I
lived into
your unthinkable death
is a splinter
of that selfsame grief,
infinitely smaller but
the same in kind:

one
stretching the mind's fibers to touch
eternal nothingness,
the other
tasting, in fear, the
desolation of
survival.

Philip Levine

Born in Detroit, Michigan in 1928, Philip Levine received his B.A. and M.A. from Wayne State University and his M.F.A. from Iowa University. He also held a poetry fellowship at Stanford University. Levine draws his poetic inspiration from the people he met while working in factories and from childhood memories of living in an industrial environment. *Selected Poems* (1984) and *Sweet Will* (1985) are his latest poetry collections. He has also helped translate the poetry of Jaime Sabines and Gloria Fuertes. Levine's many honors include the Frank O'Hara Memorial Award, the Academy of Arts and Letters Award, and grants from the Guggenheim Foundation and the National Endowment for the Arts. He has taught at California State University since 1958.

Sweet Will

The man who stood beside me
34 years ago this night fell
on to the concrete, oily floor
of Detroit Transmission, and we
stepped carefully over him until
he wakened and went back to his press.

It was Friday night, and the others
told me that every Friday he drank
more than he could hold and fell
and he wasn't any dumber for it

so just let him get up at his
own sweet will or he'll hit you.

"At his own sweet will," was just
what the old black man said to me,
and he smiled the smile of one
who is still surprised that dawn
graying the cracked and broken windows
could start us all to singing in the cold.

Stash rose and wiped the back of his head
with a crumpled handkerchief and looked
at his own blood as though it were
dirt and puzzled as to how
it got there and then wiped the ends
of his fingers carefully one at a time

the way the mother wipes the fingers
of a sleeping child, and climbed back
on his wooden soda-pop case to
his punch press and hollered at all
of us over the oceanic roar of work,
addressing us by our names and nations—

"Nigger, Kike, Hunky, River Rat,"
but he gave it a tune, an old tune,
like "America the Beautiful." And he danced
a little two-step and smiled showing
the four stained teeth left in the front
and took another suck of cherry brandy.

In truth it was no longer Friday,
for night had turned to day as it
often does for those who are patient,
so it was Saturday in the year of '48
in the very heart of the city of man

where your Cadillac cars get manufactured.
In truth all those people are dead,
they have gone up to heaven singing
"Time on My Hands" or "Begin the Beguine,"
and the Cadillacs have all gone back
to earth, and nothing that we made
that night is worth more than me.

And in truth I'm not worth a thing
what with my feet and my two bad eyes
and my one long nose and my breath
of old lies and my sad tales of men
who let the earth break them back,
each one, to dirty blood or bloody dirt.

Not worth a thing. Just like it was said
at my magic birth when the stars
collided and fire fell from great space
into great space, and people rose one
by one from cold beds to tend a world
that runs on and on at its own sweet will.

Lyn Lifshin

Born in 1942 in Burlington, Vermont, Lyn Lifshin received a B.A. from the University of Vermont in 1963. She has done graduate work at Brandeis University and at the State University of New York at Albany. Lifshin was poet-in-residence at Mansfield State College, a writing consultant for the New York State Mental Health Department, and the director of the Albany Public Library Workshop. Her poetry has appeared in hundreds of magazines and in over forty books. *Kiss the Skin Off* (1985) won the Jack Kerouac Award. Her other honors include the Hart Crane Memorial Award, residencies at the Yaddo and McDowell artist colonies, and the title of Bread Loaf Scholar.

All the Women Poets I Like Didn't Have Their Fathers

I'm thanking you
Ben for letting me
be one too I
never could say
father and still
have trouble calling
anybody love. When
a man touches my
skin I just
think of bed (no
one has ever said I

wasn't sexy) Thank
you father (the one
place you are) and
for never letting
me know I was
pretty, for
making me need
paper to say
love. We
never talked and
last week I met
someone I wanted,
I couldn't let
him know.
Now I dream I
write him too and the
letters come back
stamped rejected.
There's not much
I trust. I know
you know what
that's like—with
your secret stock
market news scribbled
in books like poems
you couldn't show
anyone
looking at trees
alone too you
sat and watched
chestnuts drop
into the snow
Even with special
glasses my eyes
need prisms to
bend things.

Still I'm sorry I never
saw what you were,
what Russian pines
blew behind your
eyes that house of
chicken and goose
feathers dissolving
like the print of
your head finally
from the gold chair.
No one understood
why you would have
sliced us out of
your will wanting
your stocks to go on
like an eternal
flame some self
investing memorial
a space ship
knocked out of
orbit flashy
untouchable
as you were
except here where
I try to add the
pieces up like each
meal you paid for on
vacation in cape
cod in a small
notebook you kept
close to your
heart with those
pills. Like that
space ship there
was a place
neither of us

could reach that
still circles
and haunts

Nathaniel Mackey

Born in Miami, Florida in 1947, Nathaniel Mackey grew up in California. He has taught at the University of Wisconsin and at the University of Southern California, and he is currently teaching at the University of California at Santa Cruz. In addition to *Eroding Witness* (University of Illinois Press: 1985), which was selected for publication by the National Poetry Series, Mackey has also authored two chapbooks: *Four for Trane* and *Septet for the End of Time*. *Bendouin Handbook*, first volume of an ongoing work entitled *From a Broken Bottle Traces of Perfume Still Emanate*, has been published in 1986 by the Callaloo Fiction Series. Mackey is editor of the literary magazine *Hambone*, and in 1986 he received an editor's grant from the Coordination Council of Literary Magazines "in recognition of excellence and innovation."

You will live more than millions of years, an era of millions,
But in the end I will destroy everything that I have created,
The earth will become again part of the Primeval Ocean . . .

—Atum to Osiris, *The Book of the Dead*

The Phantom Light of All our Day
for Jess

I wake up standing before a scene I stood
    before as a child. What bits of
     it I see no more than seem they were

ever there, though they'd
someday blur the broken paste-up
world
I saw
would blow itself apart . . .

My back to the wall whose beginning
the day of my release brought forward, so
unlikely a start, I stand watching the
brook I stood before as a boy, no sweeter
tooth but for boundaries, bite
off more
than I can chew . . .
Bittersweet kiss
of this my tightlipped muse, puckered
skin of the earth as though
its orbit
shrunk.
Shrill hiss of the sun so
much a doomsday prophet gasping voiceless,
asking,
When will all the killing
stop?

As though the truth were not so visibly
Never.
As though the light were not all but
drowned in the Well to be uncharted
East I sought . . .
Let its blue be
my heavenly witness, I resolve before
the brook
I stood before as a child . . .

Up at dawn every day these

days, I'm learning to look into
the lidlessness the North Wind
wakes . . .
learning to gaze into the sky
my invented eyes unveil under
acid rain, chemical sunsets, blush
of a
shotgun bride.

The grass blowing east at the
merest mention of wind where
there is no wind, no place for
a horse in this the riderless
world.
I'm learning to paint. I repeat
these words as an irritable mystic, my
would-be hum, neither life
nor limb not on the edge of
dislocation, some such
dance

I dare . . .
But still I stand before
the brook I stood before as a boy.
Thicknesses of paint, as if
the eye
looked into its looking, let the skull
show thru, show the Kings of
Xibalba play with poison gas and me
among them, 1940s' chemical
warfare corps . . .

I'm learning to see, says my enamored mage, what's
going on. I hear the rumbling in the music I
paint.

Luminous breezes locked in the nucleus'
inmost reaches echo Atum's vow. These
        radiant winds obey the abandon our
learning sought.

I stand watching the brook I stood before
        as a boy, the painted echo of
        a snapshot my father took. The oils
                                        thicken
my sleep,
        the unprootable oath I wake up to,
                                        the earth
a part of Ocean
                again

Michael McClure

Born in 1932 in Maryville, Kansas, Michael McClure was raised in both Washington and Kansas. After attending Tucson University for a year, he moved to San Francisco and took part in that city's "poetic renaissance." By 1955 he was reading his poetry with such well-known poets as Gary Snyder and Allen Ginsberg. His first book, *Passage*, was published in 1956. He has since written over forty books of poetry, most recently *Specks*, and over twenty plays. In 1975 McClure received a Rockefeller Fellowship for Drama, and in 1978 *Josephine* won an Obie for best play. His poetry has appeared in such magazines as *The Nation*, *Poetry*, and *Origin*.

On The Mountain
Where We Slept

IS A CITY
OF FOXES.

THEY ARE SPACED
SO THAT

their
barkings

touch
and the edges

165

of their
wanderings

meet
also.

They see
moonlight

through
the scented laurels.

They view nightshadows

of

blue-green boulders

&

smile to

yellow wildflowers

in

starlight!

So,

also

we have done that

And *see* our hands

and feet

are paws!

The densities of solids are fascinating.

§

Moonlight shining through the bay tree makes spots of
light that resemble stars in the black sky.

Robert McDowell

Born in Alhambra, California in 1953, Robert McDowell received a
B.A. in writing from the University of California at Santa Cruz and
an M.F.A. in poetry from Columbia University. An assistant
professor at Indiana State University at Evansville for six years,
McDowell has also taught at the University of California at Santa
Cruz and at Cabrillo College. With Mark Jarman, he has been
co-editor and co-publisher of *The Reaper* and the Story Line Press
since 1980. McDowell has also served as a consultant to the M.F.A.
program in writing at the University of California at Santa Cruz. He
is now an associate editor at McGraw-Hill. *Quiet Money* (Henry
Holt: 1987) is his first full-length collection.

Quiet Money
for Randy & Carole McDowell

The bootlegger opens his eyes and stares
Down the grey runway, another Wednesday.
Boney, shivering in early bathroom weather,
He locates a glass of rye on the window ledge
And flicks on the light. Flight day.
The weather report on the wireless is good,
Though what he sees in his shaving mirror
Makes him think of mechanical foul-ups—
A slice of wing shooting past him,
Chips of propeller smacking his goggles.

Flicking his thumb across the straight razor
Joe tells himself it's good to feel the edge,
To remember it's only a membrane
That separates blood from the body intact.
He thinks of landing an office job and laughs.
He thinks of coffee in a field cup and he's warm.
Down in the alley two cats howl,
The soundtrack of a skirmish. A trashcan topples.
"That's motivating music," he says,
And mutters the closing bars of "Over There"—

we won't come back until it's over over there . . .

*

Mirabelle sulks in a luncheonette on Fourth,
Daubing her nose with a hankie, stirring eggs.
She wants him. She wants him everywhere.
On the bus to work she thought of telling him
"Give it up or stop coming around,"
But the words were too heavy to carry,
Like too much weight in her handbag
Throwing off her natural stride.

Now she laughs
At the thing she'd tried last night,
Pouring so many martinis, hoping he'd nosedive
Into sleep and miss this day.
But Joe can hold his liquor
And he'd chattered all night about poets and the war.
Later, filing claims at the office,
Mirabelle can't fix on the hour she passed out,
Or the hour he pinned the note to her pillow:

See you Monday, Doll.
With something pretty from Oslo!

*

The airstrip flags point east at a quarter to five.
Joe rubs a compass in his flight jacket pocket,
His fingers brushing the pages of Rupert Brooke,
And he's thinking of wings.
Not those of machines but of birds,
What he'd wanted as a child
Who had loved the bird's life of excess
And dramatic death down a chimney
Or in the talons of a larger bird.
Walking round the plane he whistles

The Yanks are coming, the Yanks are coming . . .

"Nobody knows," he says, "but some Norwegian 3,600 miles
   away.
'Nobody crosses The Pond alone,' the experts say.
Well, I won't be rubbing their noses in it,
Though there's plenty gearing up to do just that.
Circus flyboy stuff. There's money in it,
But fame comes, too, a suit you can't take off."

He lingers, checking the Wright Whirlwind engine.
The tailwind says *look out;*
His patience says *take off.*
Far to the north the lights of Jersey sparkle,
Calming down.

Over there, over there . . .

He scrambles up on the wing, his perch,
One step from home. The cockpit
Makes him think of the backyards of boyhood.
Clearing the trees at the field's far edge
Joe banks to the left, circling a hill,

And levels out heading northeast.
He likes that initial turn, getting the feel of it,
Feeling the earthbound tug slip away.

He imagines gunning for stars,
But the stars are at peace, in collusion.
The sun balloons above the waterline;
The moon drops down to the sea.
Joe thinks of the money he's flying,
Of gin crates stacked in a hanger in Norway.
He thinks of a present for Mirabelle,
Of the life he's making, up here, among prosperous currents.

*

She doesn't want to think of him all day,
But superstition bites. She takes off,
Daydreaming herself into flight beside him.
''Joe,'' she thinks, ''the only thing I want is a home
With you on the sofa, drinking a soda.''
After five, plodding home, her head
Keeps lifting toward a drone that isn't there.
''Monday isn't far,'' she tells herself.

*

Joe's gruff Norwegian contact waves
As he lifts off, climbing in the wind
That will take him back to the luncheonette.
He climbs with the current inside him,
The current Mirabelle loves him for and fears.

Twelve hours out, twenty from home,
He fights it,
The drone of the motor stirring sleep.
He regrets staying up last night until two

Singing war songs, talking baseball
And drunk Norwegian poets and women—always women.
Joe nods behind his controls,
But something besides sleep isn't right.
Something in the sky is wrong.

He comes to long enough to focus
On a silvery image below him, skimming the sea.
Bird, then *dolphin*, occur to him. The *plane*.
That can't be, so he tells himself *reflection*
And conjures the creature from an old story
That snatches plane and pilot
If they fly too close to water.
"That can't be anyone but me," he says.
The image below him fades, heading the other way.
That's wrong. So he cups his hand outside
To catch a breeze and deflect it into his face,
But sleep blows through him, too.

Now he's hunting for the brainstorm gadget he'd installed
Under his seat. He finds it, grazes the live wire
With his wrist and sits up, back to himself.
And alone—as it should be.
Below him nothing angles but the sea.
Hitting fog he pulls back on the throttle
(Like flying inside a glass of milk)

    say a prayer, say a prayer . . .

Until he hits clear air at 4,500 feet.
He thinks of Mirabelle asleep
And of Brown and Alcock
Teaming up for the first crossing in 1919.
He thinks of them losing their bearings in fog,
Flying upside down within 500 feet of the sea.
How many times did Brown crawl out on the wing,

Wiping snow and sleet from the fuel gauge? Joe smiles.
"Those clowns made good, all right, but what for?
10,000 pounds, knighthood,
And Alcock dead in a crack-up six months later."

   Goodnight, Irene, goodnight . . .

Joe tips his wing to Alcock
And levels out over the coast of Newfoundland.

                              *

Sweeping cups from the counter into a tray,
Madge winks as Joe saunters past the register.
Mirabelle, raising a fork, freezes,
Riding out a tremor, and a wedge
Of lemon meringue free-falls to her lap.
"You can't have this and wear your food," he says.
One hand rests on her shoulder;
The other sets a hatbox on the table.
Tapping the left side of his jacket
He lowers his voice: "Tonight," he says,
"I'll show you what I got in here."
Mirabelle's face is like clearing weather
As she preens herself in the mirror,
Admires the way she looks in a smart Norwegian bonnet.
"Maybe in that hat you'll see things other ways," Joe says.
Mirabelle sits down.
Joe fidgets with a cup.
"You don't look well," she says. "What's up?"

   "I pushed it to the limit on this run.
I let myself stay up all hours
And then I couldn't hold it off—
The Sandbag Eye—I saw things.
I saw the creature from that story you hate;

I saw myself as a child, grounded in a strange neighborhood.
I saw another plane, Belle. A reflection, I guess,
But that's what shook me most. Listen,
I got a bonus for the quick turn-around.
It's more than we've ever seen.
Why don't we get hitched?
Just don't make me give it all up.''

''I know,'' she says,
And hammers one hard kiss across his chapped lips.

On the street Joe feels the slap of a newsboy's cry:

> *Lindbergh Lands In Paris*

He whistles like a punctured tire.
Mirabelle hugs his arm and nods.
''I didn't want to bring it up,'' she says.
Joe leans against a lamppost, staring east.

''Lindbergh.
I never thought he'd beat them,
Byrd and the others with all their cash.
I knew he was in the hunt, in a quiet way,
But I never figured this.
I guess I thought he was too much like me.
He'll get the tickertape parades and medals,
Money and keys to the mayor's w.c.
Think of it, honey. All that brotherly love.''

On the landing, at the door to her walk-up,
Mirabelle fumbles in her purse for keys.
''Lindbergh's never landed *here*,'' Joe says.
Inside he pulls a bottle from his duffel bag.

"Sometimes a proud man
Doesn't wave himself around.
Headlines cut the pants off privacy.
They make you public, a pioneer.
I wonder if he knows what he's in for?"

Joe talks and talks.
The moon pins a spotlight on his face.
Mirabelle wrings her hands and rocks,
The bottle open on the bureau-top,
But neither takes a drink.

*

Past three. Joe is flying blind, questioning.
Mirabelle's breathing is a motor in good repair.

   Over there, over there . . .

Joe hums under his partner's sleep.
"What?" she says, banking out of a dream.
"I'm thinking of getting a house in Jersey," he says,
But he's thinking of Lindbergh, too.
He's thinking of a plane below him,
Skimming the rooftops of Paris, beating him out.
"Anywhere," Mirabelle says. "Anything you want."

What *does* he want?

Nearing five Joe looks down on his body in a restless sleep.
Sprawling so he looks a little like Italy on a globe.
Out of the body a body looks that way,
A smear of papier-maché, a flare-up,
An ugly reminder on a fist of blue.
Joe, or Joe's double, wonders
If the quiet atmosphere he flew in was a cheat.

Mirabelle, asleep, looks like a separate country.
How can she make him believe in home?
In peace? Can anyone? Undertakers, maybe—
White-jacketed illusionists keeping a low profile.
Why does Joe's double escape so many nights?
Why, when he returns, does he keep
What he's found to himself,
A country inside a country, unmapped?
The questions hound Joe out of sleep,
So wrapping himself in a blanket
He gropes his way into a chair
And flicks on a reading lamp.
Slowly the room settles, focuses,
And he picks up a copy of *Lear*
To whisper the Fool's lines, his favorites.
Their sound, the way it makes him feel,
Is enough. He rides it into the afternoon.

*

On moving day they look like a couple
In a paperweight, their arms around each other.
Joe is Errol Flynn in a flight jacket;
Mirabelle's lucky hair falls down like rain.

After the movers back over the curb
And putter north, the newlyweds
Climb the fire escape for a farewell drink.
"What are you thinking?" she asks.

"Nothing. Just noticing the wind,
How it's turning nasty, how I wouldn't wait."
The winner in the paperweight dissolves;
A hard and lonely figure takes his place.

"Joe, how long before you face it,

Before you get it straight, what it means to you?''
''What are you talking about?''
''Not what,'' she says. ''Who.''

Joe faces her. ''Don't push,'' he says,
And suddenly he sees himself as memory,
His image fraying like tapestry.
''I hope you can take it,'' he says. ''Your man's obscurity.''

*

   ''Something Willy said just ticked Joe off,''
Mirabelle tells her neighbor in the backyard.
The iron fence between them soaks up heat.
''I don't know what.''

''I do,'' her neighbor says. ''Willy was carrying on
About the Yankees and the Babe.
You know how men get hot when they talk sports.
Well, Joe allowed how there were players in the Bush Leagues
Who were just as good as Ruth but never got the breaks.
Willy wasn't buying, and soon they were toe-to-toe.
Their faces got red.
The veins in Joe's neck popped out.
I noticed that just before he did it—
Threw his glass (I swear it nicked Willy's ear) in the pool.''

   ''That's when I came back out,'' Mirabelle says.
''I saw Willy's eyes get big like balloons
And Joe just turning, walking away.
He passed right by me and didn't speak,
Though I could feel anger breathing out of him.
It goes back further than the Yanks or the Babe.''

A drone out of the west breaks in
And both look up

As Mirabelle's single engine flyboy tips his wing.
Anna gurgles in her playpen.
Chug, their terrier, snoozes on a plank of sunlight.
The plane levels out, descending
Toward the airstrip a couple of miles away.
Mirabelle holds her breath. *Irrational*,
She tells herself, but she can't help it.
Only when he turns their Silver Ghost
Up the drive will the moment be enough,
His coming back in one piece
To lift Anna off his knee
And catch her as she parachutes back.

*

"I had a case of the yips for years," Joe says.
His nephew sips lemonade and nods,
Not knowing what Joe means. He lets him talk.

"After we got hitched
The weather always indicated *stay*.
So I'd scrub a couple of flights a month,
Then two a week, and pretty soon
I was on the ground more hours
Than I was logging in my plane.
Imagine what that did to me!
You never feel the same once you get out
From under weather and know it topside.
You miss the motion, the nerve-and-bone collision.

How many nights did I rock in my chair,
Spending in my head the cash I'd make
As soon as I got home safe? And *safe*—
That word would take me like a haunting
As I'd fall back knowing where I was.
I had it, yes. The Yank dream,

No rain, no sleet, no public pilot
Cutting his silver trail under me,
No flight I couldn't roundtrip in a day.
When I couldn't sleep I'd rock.
I don't know how I put her through
Those shifting moods, but Mirabelle was great.
She'd touch me—stop me, really—
'Level out,' she'd murmur,
But if she strayed too long I'd veer off course.
My throttle hand squeezed nothing,
Making fingernail imprints on its palm.

It got to where I had to face it,
The need for something to run up against,
A glass door, a garage wall,
An impassive, staring face on the front page.
Anna helped, and the dog, and this place,
But I needed more. I got it, too.
It's sad when I think of it.

You're probably too young to recall
The scene I'm thinking of. It was March of '32.
The Lindberghs had a house not far from here
Outside of Hopewell—ironic name!
The papers served up their grief with our daily bread.
We memorized photos of ladders
And footprints in the mud,
A ransom note on the windowsill.
The baby, as near as we could tell,
Was stuffed, still sleeping, in a burlap bag.
'It looks like the work of pros,' the cops said,
Which was good for the kid's sake.

And then the waiting. Ten weeks of dying,
Ten weeks of cranks and comforters,
Wheels (the cops called the crazies *wheels*) and volunteers.

I flew some for the cops, you know,
Shooting down false leads. It made me sick
Each time I landed with nothing to offer Lindbergh
But a negative shake of my head.
The look on his face will never leave me—
A mid-Atlantic look, your plane out of fuel.
The clocks ground on but didn't move;
Mail buried their house like lava.
And all for nothing. Cruelty.
The body turned up in the woods
A few miles away—and this is the awful part—
He'd been dead since that first night.
The ladder-man had dropped the burlap sack
And the baby's head struck a window ledge.
Imagine how the 'napper must have felt!

And Lindbergh. How far out,
In after-years, did he push himself to feel secure?
And the rest of us . . . how many couldn't sleep
For fear of waking without sons and daughters?
We learned to love the sounds of words
That covered us—words like *lock* and *alarm*,
And we raised you on them.
Now you can't look strangers in the eye,
And there may be things you can't even tell your closest friend.

Son, you have to lose to win.
That notion settled in with us
And we passed it on to you.
Thank God. You know what it meant to me?
My daughter safe, first of all,
And all of it, really.
I spent so many nights in her room
Just watching her sleep,
Convincing myself no gang would take her
From me—ex-flyboy, average businessman—

And suddenly I was happy.
My life's course felt fair.
I thought of fame and money, and still do,
How what we do to get them can make us sorry . . .

Send the word, send the word to beware.''

Thomas McGrath

Born on a North Dakotan farm in 1916, Thomas McGrath attended the University of North Dakota, Louisiana State University, and was a Rhodes Scholar at New College, Oxford. During World War II he served in the United States Air Force. McGrath has published many poetry collections, but he is best known for the multi-volumed work *Letters to an Imaginary Friend.* He has also written a novel, two children's books, and nearly twenty screenplays. His honors include the Amy Lowell Travelling Poetry Scholarship and fellowships from the Guggenheim Foundation and the National Endowment for the Arts. He has taught at many universities and colleges throughout America.

3. Now We Must Wake the Sleepers and Prepare for the Night Journey, fr. *Letter to an Imaginary Friend*

Now we must wake the sleepers and prepare for the night journey.
We climb the dusty grandfather stairs to the cold dark
Rooms where the children lie in the luminous sleep of childhood.
In the drift of light from below, their breaths rise up
Like ghost smokes lifting from tiny spirit fires.
Hands between thighs, heads on chests, legs bent back to buttocks,
Each curled like the brand of the Lazy 8 or the sign of infinity
They lie; each adream in the heaven of unfixed forms:

∞ ∞

182

We wrench them out of their sleep and sack them in animal skins,

And so we are ready for the journey home . . .
                                        the sleds loaded
With human freight . . .
                        (and some of us, sound asleep since
    sundown.

Will never remember this Christmas . . .
                                    except through the
    Memory Man!)

Just as we start to leave my grandmother slips me a gift:
One of her famous pomegranate cakelets thin as the Host.
A poker-chip-shaped token called (for reasons unknown)
A Persephone.
                Drops it inside my mitt.
                                    Gives me a kiss.

We go.
        Again the harness bells ring . . .
                                    and the runners skreek
On the packed-down snow of the village streets.
                                        In the after
        midnight.
In the growing dark, gravity, like a disease,
Has entered again those weathered houses that, since the dusk,
Have floated like clapboard clouds over the sailing town.
They are dragging their anchors now and the slow tolling bells—
The last!—having gathered the darkness into their iron throats—
Are nailing them into the earth again . . .
                                    three silver spikes
    At each house-corner

James Merrill

James Merrill was born in 1926 to an affluent family and was raised in New York City. He received a B.A. from Amherst College in 1947 after serving in the army during World War II. Merrill has travelled extensively, and for the past twenty-five years he has divided his time between Athens, Greece, and Stonington, Connecticut. His honors include a Bollingen Award for *Braving the Elements* (1972), *Poetry* magazine prizes and National Book Awards for *Night and Days* (1966) and *Mirabell* (1978), and a Pulitzer Prize for *Divine Comedies* (1976). His most recent collection is entitled *Late Settings*.

Topics

I. Casual Wear

Your average tourist: Fifty. 2.3
Times married. Dressed, this year, in Ferdi Plinthbower
Originals. Odds 1 to 9^{10}
Against her strolling past the Embassy

Today at noon. Your average terrorist:
Twenty-five. Celibate. No use for trends,
At least in clothing. Mark, though, where it ends.
People have come forth made of colored mist

Unsmiling on one hundred million screens
To tell of his prompt phone call to the station,
"Claiming responsibility"—devastation
Signed with a flourish, like the dead wife's jeans.

2. Popular Demand

These few deep strongholds. Each with generator,
Provisions, dossiers. It would seem the worst
Has happened, who knows how—essential data
Lost in the bright, chromosome-garbling burst.

You, Comrade, will indefinitely be resident
Of this one, with your disciplined women and staff;
You and yours of this one, Mr. President.
Grim huddles. Then a first, uncertain laugh

—Spirits reviving, as life's bound to do?
Not from dead land, waste water, sulphur sky.
Nowhere is anything both alive and blue
Except, inside your block heads, the mind's eye

Marveling up out of our common grave:
You never thought . . . Sincerely didn't think . . .
Who gave it clearance? It ransacks the cave
For you with cordial venom. Damn you, drink!

3. Caesarion

A glow of cells in the warm Sea,
Some vaguest green or violet soup
Took a few billion days to loop
The loops we called Eternity.

Before the splendor bit its tail
Blake rendered it in aquatint

And Eddington pursued a glint—
Recoil, explosion—scale on scale.

What stellar hopefuls, plumed like Mars,
Sank to provincial rant and strut,
Lines blown, within the occiput?
Considering the fate of stars,

I think that man died happiest
Who never saw his Mother clasp
Fusion, the tiny naked asp,
By force of habit to her breast.

Grass

The river irises
Draw themselves in.
Enough to have seen
Their day. The arras

Also of evening drawn,
We light up between
Earth and Venus
On the courthouse lawn,

Kept by this cheerful
Inch of green
And ten more years—fifteen?—
From disappearing.

Judson Mitcham

Born in Monroe, Georgia in 1948, Judson Mitcham was educated at the University of Georgia, where he received a Ph.D. in psychology. He has since taught psychology at Fort State College in Fort Valley, Georgia. His chapbook, *Notes for a Prayer in June*, is being published by State Street Press. Mitcham's work has appeared in such magazines as *The Georgia Review, Poetry Northwest, Prairie Schooner, Ironwood, Black Warrior Review,* and *Southern Poetry Review*. In 1985 he was a Bread Loaf Scholar.

Surviving in Tolstoy's Dream
for John Gardner

He tacks past the desk, smelling foul, like spoiled onion
and, as always, of alcohol. What he wants
since winter turned hard weeks back,
he finds right here—a place to sit where it's warm,
a bathroom anyone can use, clean water,
a trash can next to a vending machine
in the basement, and more. Other bums don't make it.
Bones wanting softness, they will flop onto sofas
which line the walls holding current magazines,
leafing through what they have grabbed, maybe *Life,*
Ebony, or *Better Homes and Gardens*. In a wink,
mouths fall slack, hands surrender, and the slick
picture books slip from their laps.
No sleeping allowed, they are ushered out.

But the man I follow, looking up from the cards,
veers toward someplace else. I would bet
his story is flawed by a flatness inside,
by the rambling, sad chapters on job, wife and blood,
jail and children, alley and rain. I have seen
how bare his eyes are, no different from the others',
as if burned clean of memory by enough
alcohol or scoured of what they've known
by a wind which returns any dawn, eager to pin
trash like last week's classifieds against
a sharp ledge or a charged fence. When he limps
from the last rank of fiction,
he takes off his camouflage army coat, carefully
lays it over the back of a straight chair
at the table he's chosen, then frees three buttons
of his outer shirt, peels off a layer of flannel,
jabs shirttails into bottle-smooth corduroys, walks
to a fountain on the far wall, guarding his book
like a full pint of Thunderbird, something which no one
would leave unattended. When he sits, grandly,
as if coming to a fine, free meal, he cracks the novel
to its heart, starts to read, lips moving, and as easily
as swilling any day's first drink, enters the dream.

Hilda Morley

Born in New York City in 1921, Hilda Morley was educated at Wellesley College and New York University. With her late husband, avant-garde composer Stephan Wolpe, she taught at the progressive Black Mountain College during the fifties. She has also taught at Queens College and at Rutgers and New York universities. Morley has published three books of poetry, most recently a collection of her work from 1955 to 1983 entitled *To Hold in My Hand*. Her poems have appeared in such periodicals as the *American Poetry Review*, *Harper's*, *The Hudson Review*, and *New Letters*. A resident at the Yaddo and MacDowell artist colonies and the Ossabaw Island Project, Morley was awarded a Guggenheim Fellowship in poetry for 1983–1984. She is also a recent recipient of the Capricorn Prize.

Egrets, Antigua

                      With what pleasure
in their own wings
               the egrets
fly together
          describing
long spirals,
            loosely sweeping,
delighting in their own ease,
                   their deliberateness
of flight—both ways
             Calm & swooping

in a state of freedom
& privacy,   they explore
their patterns,
                pushing them
a little farther always,
                        discovering
each time another
level in space,
                another
intersection possible—
                        each degree of
invention a reason for
natural pride
            Pleasure
in themselves is
what renews their freshness,
                        dipping
& floating again & again—
                        they can
make the air over,
                tireless

Howard Moss

Born in 1922, Howard Moss received a B.A. from the University of Wisconsin in 1943 and then continued his studies at Columbia University. He has taught at Vassar and Barnard colleges and at the University of California. Since 1958 he has been the poetry editor at *The New Yorker*. Moss has published many poetry collections, critical works, and humorous and satirical books for all ages. His latest book is *New Selected Poems* (Atheneum: 1985). His distinctions include a National Book Award in 1972, grants from the Ingram Merrill Foundation and the National Institute of Arts and Letters, and membership in P.E.N. His poems appear in such magazines as *The New Yorker, Poetry, Harper's*, and *The Nation*.

King Midas

1   The King's Speech

My food was pallid till I heard it ring
Against fine china. Every blesséd thing
I touch becomes a work of art that baits
Its goldsmith's appetite: My bread's too rich,
My butter much too golden, and my meat
A nugget on my plate, as cold as ice;
Fresh water in my throat turns precious there
Where every drop becomes a millionaire.

191

My hands leak gold into the flower's mouth,
Whose lips in tiers of rigid foliage
Make false what flowers are supposed to be.
I did not know I loved their warring thorns
Until they flowered into spikes so hard
My blood made obdurate the rose's stem.
My God was generous. But when I bleed,
It clogs the rosebed and cements the seed.

My dog was truly witty while he breathed.
I saw the tiny hairs upon his skin
Grow like a lion's into golden down.
I plucked them by the handfuls off of him,
And, now he is pure profit, my sculpturing
Might make a King go mad, for it was I
Who made those lively muscles stiffly pose—
This jaundice is relentless, and it grows.

I hate the glint of stars, the shine of wheat,
And when I walk, the tracings of my feet
Are affluent and litter where I go
With money that I sweat. I bank the slow
Gold-leaf of everything and, in my park,
A darkness shimmers that is not the dark,
A daylight glitters that is not the day—
All things are much less darling gilt this way.

Princess, come no closer; my tempered kiss,
Though it is royal still, will make you this
Or that kind of a statue. And my Queen,
Be armed against this gold paralysis,
Or you will starve and thinly bed alone
And, when you dream, a gold mine in your brain
Will have both eyes release their golden ore
And cry for tears they could not cry before.

I would be nothing but the dirt made loud,
A clay that ripples with the worm, decay
In ripeness of the weeds, a timid sun,
Or oppositely be entirely cloud,
Absolved of matter, dissolving in the rain.
Before gold kills me as it kills all men,
Dear Dionysus, give me back again
Ten fingertips that leave the world alone.

2   The Queen's Song

The palace clocks are stiff as coats of mail.
Time stopped; he flicked it with his fingernail.
O he was mine before he was a mine
      Of gold.

Time's twelve cold sentinels so grimly still
No longer chime their golden interval.
O he was love before he was the love
      Of gold.

What treasurer is this, come to my bed,
Whose suppleness is now a golden rod?
O he was King before he was the King
      Of gold.

3   The Princess' Speech

I praise the bird, the river, and the tree.
One flies, one flows, and one has made me see
That, standing still, the world is turning me.

I cannot fly. Birds carry in the morn.
I cannot flow. A river bed is born.
I grow. My leaves are green, and gold, and torn.

Divided into two, I am a tree.
The branches are too high for me to see,
The roots too hidden from reality.

They say that veins of gold lie underground.
Beware, explorers, of the spoil you find:
Though you sail back and forth, you sail around.

The laurel grows upon the laurel tree.
Apollo plucked the string of mystery
And made a golden echo in the sea.

4   The Queen's Speech

May every child of mine be barren, golden!
May every beast become a golden swine!
Here is a list, O gardeners and huntsmen,
Of what to kill and what to leave alone:
All natural things must go excepting those
That are by nature golden. Whatever grows
The King's touchy color let live, but close
Your nets upon the pink and crimson rose.

But I will save one rose tree in this pot
That I may gaze at it, and when he's not
About, I'll look and look till light is gone
At flower, petal, stem, and leaf. And then,
I'll ponder how a King became a fool!
Long live King Midas! And the Golden Rule!

5   The Huntsman's Song, The Gardener's Refrain

Is it the hawk or hare,
Blindly alive to feed,
The daylight rises for?
I have seen both bleed,
Yellow and dead.

Is it the clang of war
I waken to instead
Of the hunt as heretofore?
That shot was in my head,
Yellow and dead.

The quarry goes before.
The hunter must be fed.
I know the huntsman's lore.
I know that blood is red,
Yellow and dead.

Nature cannot bear
To gild its marriage bed
With gold that is not there.
The golden goose is dead,
Yellow and dead.

6   Address by Dionysus

There is no meekness in my sun.
It is more dazzling than the one
You cannot look at, Midas. Run
    This way or that, it follows you,
    And is indifferent to the view.

A king especially must live
Without a God's prerogative.
We take, for every gift we give,
    Two back. Your gold made you a fool.
    Now you grow wise, but in my school.

There is a lesson children learn:
You reach your hand out, and you burn.
It is no lesson kings can spurn.

Mine is a cruel curriculum
Not fit for the powerless or dumb.

Go to the river. Dip your hand
Into its silver rumblings. Stand
Still while the precious contraband
    You glitter with flows from your skin
    Till water sucks away your sin.

It is through will, and only will,
Pleasure unearths the sensual.
The Gods grind error in a mill
    Whose gold wheels turn all costly wit
    Into its dreaded opposite.

7   The Princess' Song

See how they love me,
Green leaf, gold grass,
Swearing my blue wrists
Tick and are timeless.

See how it woos me,
Old sea, blue sea,
Curving a half moon
Round to surround me.

See how it wants me,
High sky, blue sky,
Letting the light be
Kindled to warm me.

Yet you rebuke me,
O love, love I
Only pursue. See
How they love me!

8   The King's Song

What I loved most most moved me.
Tell me, soul, where now your motion is.
Looking back, I look on Orpheus,
Who, looking back, looked on Eurydice.

His voice is distant as the shelled sea.
She, underground, is where no music is.
They moved me most who loved me.
Tell me, flesh, where now your motion is.

I, an ancient King, walk blindly.
I break on pleasure where no pleasure is.
Looking back, I look on Orpheus,
Who, looking back, looked on Eurydice.

9   Dionysus' Song

Midas in the street
Makes statues out of men.
When man and money meet,
Beware! The worst is then.

Beware! The worst is then.

When animal and angel
Meet on a common ground,
And elegance is natural,
Nothing is so profound.

Nothing is so profound.

10   The King to the Princess, at the River Bank

My daughter, the river flows down to the sea.
All things begin in its rich nursery.
If you should shed a tear, shed it for me.

Remember me for this: if you should gain
What men most wish for, give it back again,
Before the Gods transform it into pain.

Stay here beside me while I dip my hand
Into the cold river. Until water end,
Pactolus, from this day, runs golden sand.

Howard Nemerov

Born in New York City in 1920, Howard Nemerov was educated at the Fieldston School and at Harvard University, where he received his A.B. in 1941. He then served four years in the Royal Canadian Air Force and the United States Air Force where he achieved the rank of first lieutenant. In 1945 he took his first teaching position at Hamilton College, and he has since taught at Bennington College, Brandeis University, and Washington University where he is currently the Edward Mallinckrodt Distinguished University Professor. Nemerov, a Consultant in Poetry at the Library of Congress for the year 1963–1964, is known for his fiction writing as well as for his poetry. He has won numerous awards, including a Guggenheim Fellowship, a National Endowment for the Arts Grant, a National Book Award, and a Pulitzer Prize. His most recent book of poetry is *Inside the Onion*.

Poetics

You know the old story Ann Landers tells
About the housewife in her basement doing the wash?
She's wearing her nightie, and she thinks, "Well hell,
I might's well put this in as well," and then
Being dripped on by a leaky pipe puts on
Her son's football helmet; whereupon
The meter reader happens to walk through
And "Lady," he gravely says, "I sure hope your team wins."

A story many times told in many ways,
The set of random accidents redeemed
By one more accident, as though chaos
Were the order that was before creation came.
That is the way things happen in the world,
A joke, a disappointment satisfied,
As we walk through doing our daily round,
Reading the meter, making things add up.

In Memory of the Master Poet Robert Browning

Remembering that century and the one before
That seemed such inexhaustible springs of song,
Di quell'amor and *Dove sono* and the rest,
Orpheus wondering what he'd do without
Eurydice, the stuffed shirts in the stalls
Sobbing about Violetta, *croce e delizia*,
Coughing her love away, where did it go,
That wonderful stuff still with us now
But as a relic, the way they used to feel
Back then about Dreyfus, about Sedan,
La Gloire, Rhine Maidens with their swimming tits
Behind the scrim, now how could that have changed
And gone beyond our caring and our care?

When things are over that's what they are, over.
Master, I too feel chilly and grown old.
Like Ike said, he that conquered Europe, things
Are more like they are now than they ever were before.

Lorine Niedecker

Born in Fort Atkinson in 1903, Lorine Niedecker was virtually
unknown to the public at the time of her death in 1970. Although her
work had been highly acclaimed by such poets as William Carlos
Williams, Kenneth Rexroth, and Robert Duncan, Niedecker lived an
isolated life, spending much of it in a cabin in a small town on Black
Hawk Island, Wisconsin. There she supported herself by working in
a print shop as well as in a hospital, scrubbing floors and cleaning
kitchens. *The Granite Pail: The Selected Poems of Lorine Niedecker*
(North Point Press: 1985) is her most recently published collection.

Easter

A robin stood by my porch
        and side-eyed
            raised up
                a worm

Alice Notley

A native Californian, Alice Notley was born in 1945. She received a B.A. from Barnard College in 1967 and an M.F.A. from the University of Iowa in 1969. It was at the University of Iowa that she met her husband, the late poet Ted Berrigan. Notley now lives with her two sons in New York City, where she gives writing workshops at the St. Mark's Poetry Project. She has published over a dozen books, most recently *Margaret & Dusty* (Coffe House Press: 1985). Her honors include the San Francisco Poetry Center Award in 1982 for *How Spring Comes* and the Coordinating Council of Literary Magazines' General Electric Foundation Award for Younger Writers in 1983.

Song Book

           to everybody.
      Why don't you think of a solution
   to my problems that's amenable
      to me? You can't. You're all
      failures. So I have to do it
      myself & make you disbelieve
      my truth. I'm tired of this

      poem. I don't want you to give me
   everything I want you to help
      me think better. That's a lie. I
      don't want to think. I don't want

to be given things. I want to be
 given. Anyone can give me.
   Give me. Give

   you. It's bad to love tightly. You
could give me to you if I didn't
   have to be you to suit your desires.
   You want to give you to you—
      that's a platitude I heard in a
      truth book that everyone read.
   I don't believe it but do I
   love you? It's not that I try
   but that I find myself
      caught in an air with you without
         my picture

         anyone anywhere love, but we don't
   have hardly anything to eat
   except of self, strange hot fall
      don't eat me dears I'm doing
         that well myself, not
            being given. Leave me alone
   don't leave me alone

   to whom am I speaking to? blue,
blue wings. (No faces.) Don't tell me a thing.

Sharon Olds

Born in San Francisco, California in 1942, Sharon Olds studied at Stanford University and at Columbia University. Her first book, *Satan Says*, received the 1981 San Francisco Poetry Center Award. *The Dead and the Living*, published three years later, was chosen as the Lamont Selection of the Academy of American Poets. Olds was also the recipient of the New York State Creative Artists Public Service Grant in poetry and grants from the National Endowment for the Arts and the Guggenheim Foundation. She currently lives in New York City.

In the Hospital, Near the End

Suddenly my father lifted up his nightie, I
turned my head away but he cried out
Share!, my nickname, so I turned and looked. He was
sitting in the cranked-up hospital bed with the
gown up around his neck
so I could see the weight he had lost. I looked where his
solid ruddy stomach had been and I
saw the skin fallen into loose
dark hairy rippled folds
lying in a pool of folds
down at the base of his abdomen, the
gaunt torso of a big man
who is dying soon. Right away I

saw how much his body is like mine, the
white angles of the hips, and then I
saw how much his body is like my
daughter's little body, the white
pelvis like a chambered shell
hollowed out on the beach. I saw the
sculptural beauty of the folds of his skin like
something poured, some rich thick matter,
I saw the rueful smile on his face,
the cast-up eyes, his innocence as he
shows me his old naked body
full of cancer, he knows I will be
interested, he knows I will find him
beautiful. If you had ever told me I'd
sit by him and he would pull up his nightie and I'd
love him, his body filled with death and his
desire to share that body, if you had
told me I would see the dark
thick bud of his penis in all that
dark hair and just look at him as I
look at my children, in love and wonder,
I would not have believed you. But now I can still
see the tiny snowflakes, white and
night-blue, on the cotton of the gown as it
rises the way we were promised at death it would rise,
the veils would fall from our eyes, we would know everything.

Brenda Marie Osbey

Born in 1957, Brenda Marie Osbey is a native of New Orleans, Louisiana. After attending Dillard University, Universite Paul Valery, and the University of Kentucky, she taught French and English at Dillard University. Osbey was curator and researcher for the Louisiana Division of the New Orleans Public Library, specializing in Louisiana's Black and Creole history and in French and Creole translations. She is a recipient of the Academy of American Poets 1980 Loring-Williams Prize and a 1984 Associated Writing Programs' 15th Anniversary Award for the poem "Portrait." Named the Bernadine Scherman Fellow of the MacDowell Colony for 1984, Osbey is a 1985–86 Fellow of the Mary Ingraham Bunting Institute of Radcliffe College. *In These Houses* (Wesleyan: 1986) is her latest book.

The Factory Poem

i don't want to whisper
somehow when i talk of feelings
some gut
seems to jump into what i say
all up in my mouth
making me wish
i had never learned to speak
remembering nunnie saying
"free yourself
clear yourself"

what did she know of freedom,
chained to some memory
of a man dead twenty or so years ago?
then again
what did she know of being down in mind
all those years
he was still singing "danny boy"
inside her head
all this time
a dead man moving around
inside her body
and her whispering to him
whenever she thought no one could hear.
i heard.
i learned love after she left
or that i'd learned it then
and just not known
because i hadn't put it to use
but i heard
and i don't want to whisper
to a man who's not there.

woman
i said i heard you
heard you had trouble in the mind
woman i heard it takes a man
to make a woman do suicide.

they used to sing it in the factory.

you have taken my keys
all the doors and windows
sing wind and rain songs
i used once to be
an airtight tunnel
complete in myself

thinking i had known
my own limits
you taught me the meaning
of words like
infinite
though once
i lived here also
now i inhabit
an empty hall
that you once made into a mansion
my furnishings are all gone
i have been drained of myself
on warm winter days
i resort to a violence
that teaches you the meaning
of words like
hurt.

what do you know of such things
i live in a factory
where other women also
manufacture blues.

i said i heard you
heard you had trouble in mind
yes i heard you
woman
i done heard you mind.

what do you know of such things
i carry dead things in me
songs and photographs
and dead flowers
i carry sand and seashells
bits of confetti,
eggshells and scribbled note paper

what do you know of such things
with all your doors and windows
sealed so neatly
against the ice and air
what do you know of whispering
inside a room with no ears at all
whispering to thin air
whispering among factory women
telling what mind really means
what do you know of seashells
and dead things
and tunnels?

and what on earth
do i know of you?

Alicia Ostriker

Born in 1937, Alicia Ostriker received a B.A. from Brandeis University in 1959 and a Ph.D. from the University of Wisconsin in 1964. She has taught at Rutgers University since 1965. Among her published works are *Songs* (1969) and *Once More Out of Darkness and Other Poems* (1974). Ostriker frequently contributes poems and criticism to many literary magazines. She received the National Endowment for the Arts Fellowship for the year 1976 through 1977. Her most recent work is a critical study entitled *Stealing the Language: The Emergence of Women's Poetry in America*.

Listen

Having lost you, I attract substitutes.
The student poets visit, think me wise,
Think me generous, confide in me.
Earnestly they sit in my office
Showing me their stigmata
Next to the Judy Chicago poster
Of her half opened writhing-petalled
Vagina that appears to wheel
Slowly clockwise when you gaze at it,
And I cry. Then they try on their ambitions
Like stiff new hiking boots, and I laugh
And approve, telling them where to climb.
They bring me tiny plastic bags
Of healthy seeds and nuts, they bring me wine,

We huddle by the electric heater
When it is snowing,
We watch the sparrows flash
And when they leave we hug.

Oh silly mother, I can hear you mock.
Listen, loveliest, I am not unaware
This is as it must be.
Do daughters mock their mothers? Is Paris
A city? Do your pouring hormones
Cause you to do the slam
And other Dionysiac dances,
And did not even Sappho tear her hair
And act undignified, when the maiden
She wanted, the girl with the soft lips,
The one who could dance,
Deserted her?

Do I suffer? Of course I do,
I am supposed to, but listen, loveliest.
I want to be a shrub, you a tree.
I hum inaudibly and want you
To sing arias. I want to lie down
At the foot of your mountain
And rub the two dimes in my pocket
Together, while you dispense treasure
To the needy. I want the gods
Who have eluded me
All my life, or whom I have eluded,
To invite you regularly
To their lunches and jazz recitals.
Moreover I wish to stand on the dock
All by myself waving a handkerchief,
And you to be the flagship
Sailing from the midnight harbor,

A blue moon leading you outward,
So huge, so public, so disappearing—

I beg and beg, loveliest, I can't
Seem to help myself,
While you quiver and pull
Back, and try to hide, try to be
Invisible, like a sensitive
Irritated sea animal
Caught in a tide pool, caught
Under my hand, can I
Cut off my hand for you,
Cut off my life.

Grace Paley

Born in 1922 in New York City, Grace Paley was raised in the Bronx by her Russian immigrant parents. Primarily known for her two books of short stories, *The Little Disturbances of Men and Women at Love* (1959) and *Enormous Changes at the Last Minute* (1974), Paley wrote poetry long before she began to write short stories. She is the recipient of a Guggenheim Fellowship, a National Council on the Arts grant, and a National Institute of Arts and Letters award. She has taught at Columbia University, Syracuse University, and is currently teaching at Sarah Lawrence College. Over the years she has been deeply involved with the women's movement and with anti-militaristic groups. Her work appears in such magazines as *The New Yorker, The Atlantic, Accent,* and *Esquire,* and her latest book is *Leaning Forward* (1985).

The Old Dog's Song

Where can I shit
             said the old dog
turning this way and that
the grasses are gone
             the asphalt is slimy with oil
on the nice rubbly lots
             there are six story buildings
where can I shit
             said the old dog
             turning this way and that

213

Where can I turn
                   said the old dog
no one is in heat
                   on this block at least
my old friends have altered
        or snap   they show me their teeth
                   not their ass
                   said the old dog
turning this way and that

This leash is so loose
                           said the old dog
turning this way and that
nobody cares if I run
                   the children have gone
the man who hangs on is like me
he looks up the block and then down
                   turning this way and that
said the old dog
                   turning this way and that

Raymond R. Patterson

Born in New York City in 1929, Raymond R. Patterson was educated at Lincoln University and at New York University. He has taught English for many years at the City College of the City University of New York. His two books of poetry are *26 Ways of Looking at a Black Man and Other Poems* and *Elemental Blues*. His work is often anthologized and appears in such magazines as *The Ohio Review*, *West Hills Review*, *The Beloit Poetry Journal*, and *The Transatlantic Review*. Patterson has performed his poetry on PBS and in Lincoln Center's Alice Tully Hall as part of the Hale Smith composition "Three Patterson Lyrics." He is the third vice-president of the Poetry Society of America and a trustee of the Walt Whitman Birthplace Association. His honors include a National Endowment for the Arts Award and a Creative Artists Public Service Fellowship.

Creative Writing

Write about what you know,
she had been told. And so
this story about her family:

her younger brother, come home,
one cold Christmas day,
from spending the night in jail;

her father, struck dumb with rage,

215

alone on his edge of the room,
sloshing gin in his beer;

her aunt, who suddenly comes,
a Christmas tree in her arms,
loudly calling their names;

her mother, assaulting the gloom
with thunderous kitchen smells,
her apron wracked with stains.

Outside, a sudden swirl
of snowflakes rattles the panes,
where tinseled angels twirl.

Somewhere a TV swells
its laughter through the walls
that close around her world.

A hiss of steam; the near,
familiar voices, distant now
and strange, as in a dream.

The anger and despair
and love her family brought her,
she must learn to bear.

She is their daughter. That is her
story—what she knows well,
what she must try to tell.

Marge Piercy

Born in Detroit, Michigan in 1936, Marge Piercy received a B.A. from the University of Michigan and an M.A. from Northwestern University. Although she has taught at the University of Kansas, the Fine Arts Work Center in Provincetown, Massachusetts, and at the State University of New York at Buffalo, where she held the Butler Chair, she chose not to make teaching her career. Nevertheless, Piercy still has made her presence felt at over one hundred colleges and universities by giving readings and leading workshops. She has published a dozen poetry collections, most recently *My Mother's Body* (Knopf: 1985), and several novels. Her honors include two Borestone Mountain Poetry Awards, a Literature Award from the Governor's Commission on the Status of Women (Massachusetts), and a fellowship from the literature program of the National Endowment for the Arts.

Nothing more will happen

You are rumpled like a sweater
smelling of burnt leaves and dried sea grasses.
Your smile belongs to an archaic boy of wasting stone
    on Delos.
You change shape like spilled mercury.
There is no part of you that touches me
not even your laugh catching like fur in your nose.

I am with you on a glacier
white snowfield gouged with blue-green crevasses
deep and the color of your eyes.
There is no place to go, we cannot lie down.
In the distance your people wait checking their gear.
We blaze like a refinery on the ice.

A dry snow begins to descend
as your hands fall clasped to your sides
as your eyes freeze to the rim of the sky.
Already I cannot see you for the snow.
Heavy iron gates like those in a levee or fortress
are closing in my breasts.

Katha Pollitt

Born in New York in 1949, Katha Pollitt was educated at Radcliffe College. Her first book, *Anarctic Traveller* (Knopf: 1982), won the National Book Critics Circle Award for Poetry. She has received fellowships from the Ingram Merrill Foundation, the Creative Artists Public Service Program, and the National Endowment for the Arts. Pollitt is the literary editor of *The Nation*.

Abandoned Poems

It's awful how they look at you: consumptives,
all eyes in their white beds,
coughing delicately into their handkerchiefs
and feebly hissing, *Don't leave us here, you bastard,*
this is your fault. What can you do but agree?
It's no use to harden your heart,
no use to explain why you had to save yourself,
still less to confess how happy you are without them,
how already you see yourself under the trees in the park:
you read the paper, you eat a ham sandwich,
then shake out the crumbs for the pigeons
and walk on, savoring
the mild autumnal air of your new country,
the kingdom of health and silence.

Milkweed

Ghost feathers, angel bones, I see them rise
over West Thirteenth Street, unearthly, shining,
tiny Quixotes sailing off to Heaven
right on schedule: it's the end of August.
I'm tired of transcendence. Let's stay home
tonight, just us, let's take the phone off the hook
and drink a peaceable beer on the fire escape.
Across the darkening garden, our lesbian neighbor
is watering her terraceful of scraggly geraniums,
the super and his wife are having a salsa party,
and in a little while the moon will rise
over the weary municipal London plane trees,
and the old classical philologist next door
will look up from his lexicon and remember
that even Zeus came down to us for love.
Love, we could do worse than listen to the city breathing
on its way to bed tonight while overhead
cold galaxies of milkweed stream and stream.

David Ray

Born in Oklahoma in 1932, David Ray received a B.A. and an M.A. from the University of Chicago. He taught at several colleges and at the Iowa Writers' Workshop. Since 1971, he had been a professor of English at the University of Missouri-Kansas City. He has published six books of poetry, most recently *The Touched Life: New and Selected Poems*, and one book of fiction. In 1987 Wesleyan University Press will publish *Sam's Book*, a collection of Ray's poems dedicated to the memory of his late son. Ray's work often appears in anthologies and magazines. He is an editor as well, with the literary quarterly *New Letters* and several anthologies to his credit. He has produced the weekly national radio program ''New Letters on the Air'' and has travelled throughout North America and Europe reading his poems and giving lectures. Ray won the Poetry Society of America's William Carlos Williams Award and five P.E.N. Syndicated Fiction Awards. In 1987 he will be the Visiting Professor of English at the University of Otago, New Zealand.

Billiards

There's a couple, live not far
from us, a corner house—
lights on all night, no curtains.
When we walk the dog at 2 a.m.
they're still at it, the billiards
they were playing when we drove by
not much past 8. Fact is,

221

day and night, noon too
they're playing billiards, that table
taking up their entire living
room—and I so admire
their dedication, which few have
to their art or ecstasy, I want
to knock and tell them so, join
the game perhaps! It's so important
to have an interest,
something one's intent upon.
I fetch the dog lead, envy
his leaping up, high as a starved fish
toward gleaming jungle leaves,
wish we desired in life
something as much as he does
his little walk, sniffing at grass,
or the joy of their billiards,
green baize lawn bent to,
stick in hand, brow
like a plowed field furrowed.

A Couple of Survivors

He was a G.I. and she was huddled with the others
in their zebra suits, in a tin warehouse waiting
to be shot, all women and girls, when the noises
outside closed in and the shouts were not German
and the tin door slid open—a man framed in light.
She was the first to step out, into the sun
and he was there with his rifle, an American,
struck dumb, cagey, still looking about for the guards
who had run into the forest, and she said in German
I am a Jew and he said I am too, from Brooklyn, New
York, and he smiled, politely. And then, as she
now tells it, he asked if she would show him the others.
And with one gesture, the way she puts it,
he restored her to humanity. After those years,
the terrible years, he restored her
by taking one step back, waving her on,
letting her precede him, into the warehouse
where the women and girls stood, staring.
Now they are Americans and there are the two sides
to the memory, the captain sliding open that door
of the warehouse, the sixteen year old girl
the first out, the meeting, the joy
of the first smile on the stunned face, and the other.

Mary Jo Salter

Born in 1954 in Grand Rapids, Michigan, Mary Jo Salter studied at Radcliffe College and at Cambridge University. Her poetry has appeared in *Poetry, The New Yorker*, and *The Kenyon Review*. *Henry Purcell in Japan* is her first poetry collection. Salter has also published criticism in *The New Republic* and *The Atlantic Monthly*, where she was a staff editor. An instructor of English at Harvard University and Mount Holyoke College, Salter spent 1980 through 1983 in Japan teaching English as a foreign language at such institutions as the Asahi Culture Center. Her many honors include prizes from the Academy of American Poets and the Discovery/*The Nation* Competition, a National Endowment for the Arts Fellowship, and election to P.E.N. Married with one child, she currently lives in London.

On Reading a Writer's Letters

At last we have a picture of her life—
more colorful than honest, as her trade
led her to value more the thing that's made
than what it's made of. One must wonder if
even a scribbled postcard's a first draft,
knowing the curse that forced her to revise;
and once she coined a phrase, she spent it twice.
Her correspondents variously were left

with lines of a character nobody knew
wholly except herself, perhaps, whose talent
shows finally that self in overview:
she is this artifice, we'd say, if we
her readers, unacquainted but omniscient
narrators, were asked to tell her story.

Refrain

But let his disposition have that scope
As dotage gives it.
                              —Goneril to Albany

Never afflict yourself to know the cause,
said Goneril, her mind already set.
No one can tell us who her mother was

or, knowing, could account then by the laws
of nurture for so false and hard a heart.
Never afflict yourself to know the cause

of Lear's undoing: if without a pause
he shunned Cordelia, as soon he saw the fault.
No one can tell us who her mother was,

but here's a pretty reason seven stars
are seven stars: because they are not eight.
Never afflict yourself to know the cause—

like servants, even one's superfluous.
The King makes a good fool: the Fool is right.
No one can tell him who his mother was

when woman's water-drops are all he has
against the storm, and daughters cast him out.
Never afflict yourself to know the cause;
no one can tell you who your mother was.

Gjertrud Schnackenberg

Born in Tacoma, Washington, Gjertrud Schnackenberg received a B.A. from Mount Holyoke College in 1975. *Portraits and Elegies* (1982) is her first poetry collection. Her poems have been anthologized and appear in such magazines as *Anataeus, The New Yorker, The Paris Review, The Atlantic Monthly, Harper's,* and *Poetry.* She served as a panelist for the National Endowment for the Arts, recommending poets for 1984 fellowships, and has read her works widely in the United States and abroad. Her many honors include the Amy Lowell Travelling Poetry Scholarship and *The Paris Review*'s Bernard Conners Prize.

Sonata
Overture

More loudly to inveigh against your absence,
Raising the volume by at least a third,
Humbly I say I've written this immense
Astonishing "Sonata" word by word,
With leitmotivs you'll wish you'd never heard,
And a demented, shattering Cadenza.
I'm pained to say that scholarship insists
Cadenzas are conclusion to Concertos,
Not Sonatas—true Sonatas close
With what pedantic musicologists,
Waving their Ph.D.s beneath my nose,
Persist in calling Recapitulation.

My double ending is a Variation:
I couldn't choose between them once I chose
To write two endings, so, because I wrote a
Recapitulation and Cadenza,
My piece concludes two times—and then it ends
Again because I've added on a Coda.

To brush up on Sonata structure: first,
The Exposition sounds two melodies,
Deeply dissimilar, in different keys,
Major and minor. Part Two is a burst
Of brainstorms scholars call Development,
In which the two themes of the Exposition
Are changed and rearranged past recognition,
Distorted, fragmented, dissolved, and blent
Into chromatic superimposition,
Till, imperceptibly, two themes unite.
And then, if everything is going right,
The piece concludes in Recapitulation.

Exposition

Theme One: My life lacks what, in lacking you?
Theme Two: Does the material world exist?

(Ideally your neurons should resist,
As yet, connecting Numbers One and Two.
But note the skill, the frightening mastery,
The lunatic precision it entails
To merge these separate themes, the way train rails
Converge as they approach infinity.)

Development

I dreamed that an encyclopedia
Opened before my eyes and there I found
Analogies to sort of stack around
My what-is-life-without-you-here idea:

Like *nous* detached from Anaxagoras,
Like cosmic fire glimmering without
A Heraclitus there to find it out,
Like square roots waiting for Pythagoras,
Like One-ness riven from Parmenides,
Like Nothing without Gorgias to detect it,
Like paradox sans Zeno to perfect it,
Like plural worlds lacking Empedocles,
Like Plato's chairs and tables if you took
The furniture's Eternal Forms away,
Objects abandoned by Reality
Still look the same, but look the way things look
When I behold my life without you in it:
A screwy room where chairs and tables lack
Dimension from the front, the side, the back,
Like finity without the infinite,
Where tea parties are held without the Hatter,
It's like a single point withdrawn from Space,
It's like a physicist who cannot trace
The ultimate constituents of matter—
There is no evidence Matter exists.
Thus do I introduce Theme Number Two.
And I can't prove it, but I know it's true:
The physical eludes the physicists.
They've chased down matter past atomic rings
Into small shadows, and they've lost it there.
It seems that they can't find it anywhere.
They stalk imaginary floating things
Like amateurish lepidopterists

Round babbling brooks and mossy fairy knolls.
Their net strings map out squares of empty holes.
Behold them snatching something in their fists:
Their fingers uncurl, cautious, on the sight
Of Nothing crushed against the sweaty hand.
But then I'm prejudiced, you understand.
Not everyone on earth believes I'm right.
But lest you think I'm kidding, or perverse,
I went to hear a Lecture just last year
About some things which I hold very dear:
The smallest pieces of the universe.
The Lecturer referred to them as Quarks.
He seemed impervious to the mystery
Surrounding their invisibility.
I asked, when he concluded his remarks,
"But are Quarks physical?"
                              You'd think that he
Were someone nearly martyred and I'd said
Our duty's to die peacefully in bed.
He took his glasses off and blinked at me.
Were I John Milton, I would now destroy
This moment of high drama and deploy
A thirty-line Homeric simile.
But I'm not Milton, nor was meant to be.
He put his glasses on, and said, "Of course."

Now, I may be the south end of a horse,
But logically and analogically,
And physically, and metaphysically,
And, if it gets to that, religiously,
And absolutely scientifically,
I don't believe that Quarks can pass the test
Of Being There, and since they're fundamental,
Why, then, the world's a dream, and dreams are mental,
And since in mental matters East or West
I need you for this dream's interpretation—

Stop looking at your watch, for I've divined,
With these two themes uncomfortably combined,
It's time now for the Recapitulation.

Recapitulation

Frankly, I'm disinclined to reassert
The themes my Exposition indicated.
Stuffed-shirts there are, and hordes of overrated
Experts who would slay or badly hurt
With airy wave of hand my insights; no,
I will not play to them, I'll not rehash
My song though they with hard and cold cash
Should bribe me, or should tell me where to go.
My complex principles are explicated
Under "Development." So let them laugh:
I'll not permit this section to be half
So convoluted as anticipated.

Cadenza

Sing, Heav'nly Muse, and give me lyric flight,
Give me special effects, give me defiance
To challenge the Academy of Science
On fundamental points, and get them right;
Give me the strength to can the Latinisms,
To forge analogies between the thing
Nature abhors and my apartment; sing
To vanquish literary criticisms
If possible and literary sharks.
And even if you feel submicroscopic
Elements exceed me as a topic,
Please try to back me up regarding Quarks,
Thereby to advocate my metaphor
(Absence the vehicle, physics the tenor)
So that the Universal Void coincides

With showing—I daresay, with showing off—
The consequences of his going off;
By showing everything, in fact, but slides.

Coda

My heart detests, reviles, denounces, loathes
Your absence with a passion like a furnace.
The shirt of Love, said Eliot, will burn us;
And normally I'd add: "Love's other clothes
Burn just as badly," but good taste prevents
My introducing still another figure—
Good taste prevents this piece from getting bigger,
Lest theorists mark my brutish ignorance
Of Aristotle's golden-ruled proportion.
Line hundred forty-nine: to summarize,
Beginning with line hundred fifty-one,
How much it matters, love, that you come home—

But I've grown sensitive about this poem.
Its logic, its ideas, its sheer size
Were meant to buffalo and pulverize
Critical inquiries into its merit.
But I dislike it too; I too can't bear it;
I find it unendurably conceited,
Belligerent, high-handed, asinine;
I too can hardly force myself to read it;
Come home, before I write another line.

Philip Schultz

Philip Schultz was born in 1945 and was raised in Rochester, New York. His first book of poems, *Like Wings* (Viking: 1978), was nominated for a National Book Award and received an American Academy and Institute Award in Literature. *Deep Within the Ravine*, Schultz's second book, won the 1984 Lamont Selection of the Academy of American Poets. His other honors include a National Endowment for the Arts Fellowship. Schultz is a frequent contributor to literary magazines. He teaches creative writing at New York University and lives in Greenwich Village.

I'm Not Complaining

It isn't as if I never enjoyed good wine
or walked along the Hudson in moonlight,
I have poignant friends & a decent job,
I read good books even if they're about
miserable people but who's perfectly happy,
I didn't go hungry as a kid & I'm not constantly
oppressed by fascists, what if my apartment
never recovered from its ferocious beating,
no one ever said city life was easy, I admit
my hands turn to cardboard during love-making
& I often sweat through two wool blankets—
but anxiety is good for weight-loss, listen,
who isn't frightened of late night humming
in the walls, I don't live in a police state,

I own a passport & can travel even if I can't
afford to, almost everyone is insulted daily,
what if love is a sentence to hard labor &
last year I couldn't pay my taxes, I didn't
go to prison, yes, I've lost friends to alcohol
& cancer but life is an adventure & I enjoy
meeting new people, sure it's hard getting older
& mysteriously shorter but insomnia & depression
afflict even the rich & famous, okay, my folks
were stingy with affection & my pets didn't live long,
believe me, sympathy isn't what I'm after, I'm basically
almost happy, God in all His wisdom knows that at heart
I'm really not complaining . . .

James Schuyler

Born in Chicago in 1923, James Schuyler grew up in Washington D.C. and in Buffalo, New York. He attended Bethany College in West Virginia. During World War II, he served in the Navy and remained in Italy until 1950 when he returned to the United States, settling in New York City. Schuyler has published over ten poetry collections, most recently *A Few Days* (Random House: 1985). His book, *The Morning of the Poem* won the Pulitzer Prize for 1981. He has written plays, three novels, and criticism for *Art News*. In 1983 he was elected a fellow of the Academy of American Poets.

Moon

Last night there was
a lunar eclipse: the
shadow of the earth
passed over the moon.
I was too laze-a-bed
to get up and go out
and watch it. Besides,
a lunar eclipse doesn't
amount to much unless
it's over water or
over an apple orchard,
or perhaps a field,
a field of wheat or
just a field, the kind

where wildflowers
ramp. Still, I'm sorry
now I didn't go out
to see it (the lunar
eclipse) last night,
when I lay abed instead
and watched *The
Jeffersons*, a very
funny show, I think.
And now the sun shines
down in silent brightness,
on me and my possessions,
which I have named,
New York.

Hugh Seidman

Born in Brooklyn, New York in 1940, Hugh Seidman holds degrees in mathematics and physics, as well as an M.F.A. from Columbia University. He has published three poetry collections, most recently *Throne/Falcon/Eye* (Random House: 1982). His honors include three National Endowment for the Arts Grants, a Creative Artists Public Service Program Grant, fellowships at Yaddo and MacDowell artist colonies, and the Yale Series of Younger Poets Prize for his first book, *Collecting Evidence* (Yale: 1970). Seidman has taught writing at The New School for Social Research and at Columbia, Wisconsin, and Yale universities. He currently lives in New York City.

8.1.83

Afternoon's hundreds under the Citicorp on the platform—
feverish underworld over the molten core of the world.

I need money to learn, scrawled on a board,
as if thought literally fed the dwarf violinist's monstrous head.

But we put a dollar in his cup, grateful for his note
merged then in the heat with the train roar to West Fourth.

To Krishna's shorn battalion intoning before the cars
to the cymbal rattle on the Avenue of the Americas.

A dozen statues lined up in a box: pink baby to white skeleton—
on top of which a beast axed a cow with a human face.

Which later you said meant thought's death, as well as death—
a thought, you smiled, birthday champagne kills best.

Your lustrous glass raised once, forever, to your lips,
though even the earth shall vaporize and the sun fill space.

Gail Shepherd

Born in Reno, Nevada in 1959, Gail Shepherd received a B.A. in 1983 and an M.A. in 1985 from the University of Florida, where she studied creative writing and literature with Donald Justice, William Logan, and Dave Smith. She taught at her alma mater for two years before moving to London, England. Shepherd has spent the past year writing poetry, fiction, and travel articles, as well as exploring the city of London. Her poems have been published in *Poetry, Calliope, The Mangrove*, and *Prairie Schooner*. She is the recipient of a Phi Beta Kappa Creative Achievement Award and a Michael Hauptman Creative Writing Award.

For a Lost Child

They are closing the saw-mill down for you,
the logs are still in the river's vein,
the toothy wheel has stopped, it turns no more,
and now the swamp is sighing out your name,

wooing the dark's black heart with the lullaby
whose only word means you. You think you're nowhere;
curled in the hush beneath palmetto fans,
the cypress knees remind you of nothing, the air

holds a scent you will never forget.
All around, the swamp is full of stars.

Here is your universe, among the grasses,
crab-hole, old stump shaped like a foot, green timber

leaning in the thicket, tangle of a redbird's nest.
And there is your mother's call across the marsh,
that would reel you in like a gasping fish, out,
out of your element, and force you to exist.

Charles Simic

Born in Yugoslavia in 1938, Charles Simic came to the United States in 1949 and was raised in Chicago. He received a B.A. from New York University, where he also did his graduate work. He has taught at the University of New Hampshire since 1974. Simic frequently translates French, Russian, and Yugoslavian poetry, and he is noted for his work on the Yugoslavian poet Vasko Popa's *The Little Box* and *Homage to the Lone Wolf*. For his own poetry, Simic was awarded a Guggenheim Fellowship and a National Endowment for the Arts Grant. His latest book is *Selected Poems* (Braziller: 1985).

Happy End

And then they pressed the melon
And heard it crack
And then they ate enough to burst
And then the bird sung oh so sweetly
While they sat scratching without malice
Good I said for just then
The cripples started dancing on the table
That night I met a kind of angel
Do you have a match she said
As I was unzipping her dress
Already there were plenty of them
Who had ascended to the ceiling
Lovers they were called and they held
Roses between their teeth while the Spring

Went on outside the wide open windows
And even a stick used in childbeating
Blossomed by the little crooked road
My hunch told me to follow

Watch Repair

A small wheel
Incandescent,
Shivering like
A pinned butterfly.

Hands thrown up
In all directions:
The crossroads
One arrives at
In a nightmare.

Higher than that
Number 12 presides
Like a beekeeper
Over the swarming honeycomb
Of the open watch.

Other wheels
That could fit
Inside a raindrop.

Tools
That must be splinters
Of arctic starlight.

Tiny golden mills
Grinding invisible
Coffee beans.

When the coffee's boiling
Cautiously,
So it doesn't burn us,
We raise it
To the lips
Of the nearest
Ear.

Louis Simpson

Louis Simpson was born in 1923, in Jamaica, British West Indies, and grew up in Kingston, Jamaica. His father was a second generation Jamaican of Scottish descent, and his mother was from a family of Polish Jews. At seventeen he moved to New York and attended Columbia University. His schooling was interrupted in 1943 when he served in the U.S. Army as an infantryman, receiving two Purple Hearts and a Bronze Star. After the war he returned to Columbia University, earning a B.S. degree (1948), an M.A. (1950) and a Ph.D. (1959). He has worked as an editor and in 1957, with Donald Hall and Robert Pack, Simpson edited the highly acclaimed anthology *New Poets of England and America*. He has taught at Columbia University and the University of California at Berkeley. Since 1967 he has been professor of English at the State University of New York at Stony Brook. Simpson has received numerous honors and awards such as an American Academy of Arts and Letters Rome Fellowship, an Edna St. Vincent Millay Memorial Award, two Guggenheim Fellowships, and a Pulitzer Prize for *At the End of the Open Road*.

A Fuse Link

Here lie James and Drucilla Gordy;
Zeddock K. Evans, 1812–1863;
Hezekiah Shockley, Arabella Shockley,

and an acre of bad writing:

"Till Thy Name Shall Every Grief Remove
With Life. With Memory. And With Love."

Must love be forgotten?
O God, Horatio, what wounded names
(words standing thus misplaced) shall live behind us!

*

Can it be? Yes, it is . . .
parked by the service station.
We'll kiss and make up,
pretend it never happened.

The mechanic has something to show me
in the palm of his hand:
"This is what did it."
I stare, and he explains, "A fuse link."

A flat little piece of metal
scarcely bigger than an earring.
A fuse link. Of course, that would explain everything.

*

Goodbye to the bronze Napoleon,
the cemetery on the hill
and smoke at the heart of a valley.

It's good to be travelling again
though I'm in a single lane
behind an old Studebaker

with children in the back making faces,
holding up their Cabbage Patch dolls,
sticking out their tongues,

for so many miles
I am practically one of the family.

Dave Smith

Born in 1942 in Portsmouth, Virginia, Dave Smith received a B.A. from the University of Virginia in 1965 and an M.A. from Southern Illinois University in 1969. Before receiving his Ph.D. from Ohio University in 1976, Smith served in the U.S. Air Force from 1969 to 1972 as a staff sergeant. The author of eight books, most recently *The Roundhouse Voices: Poems 1970–85*, Smith is founding editor of *Back Door* magazine and poetry editor of *Rocky Mountain Review*. His honors include a National Endowment for the Arts Fellowship and an American Academy of Arts and Letters Award. Smith has taught at several universities, including Western Michigan and Utah universities and the College of William and Mary. He currently teaches at Virginia Commonwealth University.

On a Field Trip at Fredericksburg

The big steel tourist shield says maybe
fifteen thousand got it here. No word
of either Whitman or one uncle
I barely remember in the smoke
that filled his tiny mountain house.

If each finger were a thousand of them
I could clap my hands and be dead
up to my wrists. It was quick
though not so fast as we can do it
now, one bomb, atomic or worse,

the tiny pod slung on wingtip,
high up, an egg cradled
by some rapacious mockingbird.

Hiroshima canned nine times their number
in a flash. Few had the time
to moan or feel the feeling
ooze back in the groin.

In a ditch I stand
above Marye's Heights, the book-
bred faces of Brady's fifteen-year-old
drummers, before battle, rigid
as August's dandelions
all the way to the Potomac
rolling in my skull.

If Audubon came here, the names
of birds would gush, the marvel
single feathers make
evoke a cloud, a nation,
a gray blur preserved
on a blue horizon, but
there is only a wandering child,
one dark stalk snapped off
in her hand. Hopeless teacher,
I take it, try to help her
hold its obscure syllables
one instant in her mouth,
like a drift of wind
at the forehead, the front door,
the black, numb fingernails.

Gary Soto

Gary Soto was born in 1932 in Fresno, California, and attended Fresno State College and the University of California at Irvine. His poems often appear in such magazines as *The American Poetry Review*, *The Missouri Review*, and *Poetry*. *The Elements of San Joaquin* (1977), *The Tale of Sunlight* (1978), *Where Sparrows Work Hard* (1981), and *Black Hair* (1985) are four of his poetry collections. His many awards include an Academy of American Poets Prize as well as National Endowment for the Arts and Guggenheim Foundation fellowships. He currently teaches English and Chicano Studies at the University of California at Berkeley.

Brown Girl, Blonde Okie

Jackie and I cross-legged
In the yard, plucking at
Grass, cupping flies
And shattering them against
Each other's faces—
Smiling that it's summer,
No school, and we can
Sleep out under stars
And the blink of jets
Crossing up our lives.
The flies leave, or die,
And we are in the dark,
Still cross-legged,

Talking not dogs or baseball,
But whom will we love,
What brown girl or blonde
Okie to open up to
And say we are sorry
For our faces, the filth
We shake from our hair,
The teeth without direction.
"We're ugly," says Jackie
On one elbow, and stares
Lost between jets
At what this might mean.
In the dark I touch my
Nose, trace my lips, and pinch
My mouth into a dull flower.
Oh God, we're in trouble.

Monroe K. Spears

Born in Darlington, South Carolina in 1916, Monroe K. Spears was educated at the University of South Carolina and received a Ph.D. from Princeton University in 1940. His teaching career, which began at the University of Wisconsin, was interrupted in 1942 when Spears served as an Army and Air Force officer. In 1946 he resumed teaching and taught at Rice University from 1964 until 1986. Spears has published various critical works and has edited several collections. He edited the *The Swanee Review* from 1952 until 1961 and then remained an advisory editor for the magazine during the next twelve years. His own poems have appeared in *The Southern Review, The Hudson Review* and *The Swanee Review. The Levitator and Other Poems* is a collection of his poetry. Spears' honors include a Rockefeller Fellowship and two Guggenheim Fellowships.

A Painful Subject

I. Metamorphosis

When Gregor Samsa woke to find himself transformed
He seemed to be a large disgusting insect.
I wake daily to a more gradual transformation
Not into bug, but something equally strange and repellent,
A metamorphosis more chilling than any in Ovid.
Girl into tree or star or spider, man into stag or flower
Strange life flowing in the veins instead of blood,
This is exciting, fascinating; and even better

Stones into men, statue into living girl.
Joyce's characters seem not to mind their endless process
Flowing as they talk into rivers or hills or mythical types.
But my transition seems to be endless and painful both.
Like Gregor, I become less than human,
Possibly smelly or unpleasant,
To be hustled out of sight as quickly
     as the humans can arrange it.
To go from adult to old man
Is truly to change into another species
Apart as a lame duck, having no space in the future.

II. Palindrome

Though we have known, at least since Heraclitus,
That the way up and the way down are one and the same,
It is not often noted that there is also
Between growing up and growing old a surprising symmetry.
After sixty, as before fifteen, one's age is public knowledge
And counted in public even to fractions of a year.
One is preoccupied with sight and hearing
     and bodily functions.
In spite of fear of falling
The basic accomplishment of walking looms large and precious.
Sleep and food must be just right, and strength not overtaxed.
The adult's sense of mastery, competence, being in control
Becomes a memory. It is almost like
Reversing a film, or reversing any event in Newtonian physics
Except that it isn't funny.

III. Haydn Old, or the Joy of Aging

Unlike many a genius, Haydn was beloved:
Generous to his rivals, faithful to his wife,
Religious, hard-working, charitable and kind,
A great artist and a truly good man.

But he lived too long. After *The Seasons*
He recognized that his seasons were finished:
Nothing but Winter now; no more rebirths.
But the Spring stirrings were still there;
Ideas pursued him "to the point of torture"
Though he no longer had strength to work them out
Or even write them down. *The Seasons* finished him, he said.

What do you do after you've written *Hamlet*? Well,
If you're Shakespeare you write *Othello, Lear,* and *Macbeth*.
But even for Shakespeare, the question keeps coming up
And eventually there's no answer. He retired, of course,
But even after *The Tempest*, that greatest farewell to the stage,
He couldn't really leave it alone:
In his last years he had a hand in some dreadful hackwork.

Faulkner, when at last he won fame and money
Faced two decades of declining powers.
Einstein, early honored, lived forty years in frustration
Rejecting the quantum, pursuing the unified field.
After dazzling early success, Rossini spent forty years
Composing only a little church music.
Hawthorne spent his later years trying to write novels
That came apart in his hands.

Why can't the artist break his staff and drown his book?
Does he need his art long after it needs him?

Elizabeth Spires

Born in Lancaster, Ohio in 1951, Elizabeth Spires received a B.A. from Vassar College in 1974 and an M.A. from Johns Hopkins University in 1979. She has published two poetry collections, *Globe* (Wesleyan University Press: 1981) and *Swan's Island* (Holt, Rinehart & Winston: 1985), and her poems have appeared in *Poetry, The New Yorker*, and *The Yale Review*. Spires has been an assistant editor, a free-lance writer, and a college instructor. Her honors include a National Endowment for the Arts Fellowship, a Pushcart Prize, and the 1986 Amy Lowell Travelling Scholarship. She currently lives in London, where she is working on a third poetry collection.

Ocean City: Early March

Along Ocean Highway, apartments rise up
to ten and twenty stories,
white, hallucinatory, defying the shifting sand,
the storm moving in off the Atlantic
that drives the rain, needle-like,
across the windshield so that we can't see,
so that we stop in Ocean City to wait the storm out
at the Dutch, the only bar on the boardwalk
open this time of year, all the concessions
boarded-up, weather-beaten, closed against the
     season.

Last summer in violet light, kites
spiralled downward in loops, then up,
dragons and birds flying high above the boardwalk.
Ocean City. Haven of the lost and aimless,
with a ten-foot sand sculpture of Christ
illuminated by neon lights.
People on their way to Ripley's BELIEVE IT OR NOT
looked on in apathy, then wandered off,
their children begging for another ride
on the Avalanche or Safari.
Out, far out, at the end of a pier,
silhouetted against grey sky, grey water,
Morbid Manor hovered, a gothic image,
as children ran screaming from the exit door,
chased by a ghost with the chain saw.
One child ignored it all; she lay with her face
pressed close to a knothole in the pier,
looking down, down, to the boiling black water.
"What do you see?" I asked,
but she didn't move or answer me.
Long, narrow, and dark,
the Dutch, with its shifting clientele—
from summer weekend pickups to Ocean City regulars—
allows for strangers. We order Irish coffee,
then two more, and use our change to play an arcade game.
Aliens, half an inch high, in green armor,
drop out of a glowing sky and quickly multiply.
Our backs to the storm, we play out
old anxieties, losing each game to time and starting over:
we must save what's being threatened and not ask why.

William Stafford

Born in 1914 and raised in Kansas, William Stafford received an M.A. from the University of Kansas and a Ph.D. from the University of Iowa in 1953. He spent over two decades as a professor at Lewis and Clark College in Portland, Oregon. He also served for one year as the Consultant in Poetry at the Library of Congress. Since the 1940s, Stafford's poems have appeared in magazines; the first of his twenty poetry collections was published in 1960. His latest books are *Smoke's Way* and *Stories That Could Be True*. Among Stafford's many honors are the Shelley Memorial Award, the Melville Cane Award, and the National Book Award.

A Thought That Is Real

You came in my thought. Wind blew, rain . . .
You stayed the same. Then in my thought
you went away. In all the world
nobody cared. Nobody spoke
in all the world. They opened their mouths
and no sound came. They touched my hand
but I never felt. Then I knew this: we live
a dream, and all else is lost
when we wake to the dark. But some things
we think make real all the rest.

All the world faded when you left my thought.

Patricia Storace

Patricia Storace was born in Chicago but was raised in Mobile, Alabama. She was educated at the Medeira School, Barnard College, and Cambridge University. *Heredity*, her first book, is forthcoming from Beacon Press. Her poems have appeared in such magazines as *The Paris Review, Harper's*, and *The New York Review of Books*. Storace has been employed by the Santa Fe Opera and was managing editor of *Parnassus: Poetry in Review*. She is currently an assistant editor at *The New York Review of Books*, where she had previously been an editorial assistant. In 1981 Storace won the Arvon Poetry Contest, which was judged by Ted Hughes, Seamus Heaney, and Philip Larkin. She was a fellow at Yaddo in 1986.

A Personal Pronoun I

First among the pronouns to stand erect,
I; concentrated might, the Doric column of the alphabet,
spine of sentences, radiating verbs.
How it was in the beginning, I don't forget,
all words then, sworn courtiers, wore my signet.

Foundation of all sounds of pain or lust,
irreducible, raw in flamenco cries'
firelight refrain of wound or coupling, "Ai, ai, ai!"
crucifix of language, I precede knowing: I love, I die.

It

Little it, little eunuch, little culprit
struck match dropped that burns the house
of the five-year-old who didn't mean to do it.

Little understudy, hid behind curtains, tacit;
all that the tongue-tied point to when
they've lost the name of whatchyamacallit.

Misplaced earring, ticket, stolen loot,
the cache of emeralds the detective found
after the bandit confessed to it.

Half-wit, victim, little scapegoat;
alone and cornered by a crowd of bullies—
"Oh beat it, oh kick it, oh pummel it!"

Focus of tenderness and regret;
Peace and quiet and time will heal it,
but it's a pity, oh it's a pity, isn't it?

Little grain, olive pit, conduit
through which the world poured when God saw
that it was good; creation's seed, atom—
and infinite.

Richard Stull

Born in Ohio in 1951, Richard Stull attended the University of Cincinnati and the University of Iowa. He has been a resident at Yaddo artist colony and is the recipient of an Ingram Merrill Foundation Grant. His poetry has appeared in *Epoch, Shenandoah*, and *The Bad Henry Review*. He currently lives in New York City.

Position

Snow is falling through the lower atmosphere.
Three lights at various levels shine through the window.
A double reflection of myself appears in the glass.
Now two more lights move simultaneously beyond the frame.
A cup is picked up in the glass and applied to the lips
Of another reflection. It is returned to the book
Upon which it had been resting. The book and cup are out of
    focus.
This is caused in part by the warp of the window glass.
The book is closed. Earlier, the book lay open in my lap.
It was dusk; the light had not yet been switched on.
I remember a phrase from a page of the book.
The phrase was in French, and I translated it.
It is this translated version of the original that now
Surfaces in my mind. It is not the original phrase
Contained in the book. The phrase that I remember from the book
Does not exist in the book upon which the cup now sits.
The book is closed. The phrase I am remembering

Is a translation of one printed in the book.
This sequence of events has happened many times.
Outside, the snow is falling much harder.
The book is no longer reflected in the glass. Paper,
Cigarettes, a cup which may be empty, part of an arm:
All these things are distorted by the glass and the storm.
Beyond the window, time is passing very quickly as I write.

Henry Taylor

A native Virginian, Henry Taylor was born in 1942. He earned a B.A. from the University of Virginia and an M.A. from Hollins College. Among his poetry collections are *The Horse Show at Midnight, An Afternoon of Pocket Billiards*, and *Desperado*. He was awarded the Witter Bynner Prize in 1984 and won the Pulitzer Prize for poetry in 1986. Taylor has taught at several colleges and is currently a professor of literature at The American University. His latest book is *The Flying Change* (Louisiana State University Press: 1985). He frequently contributes to literary magazines and is a noted translator as well.

Shapes, Vanishings

1

Down a street in the town where I went
to high school twenty-odd years ago, by doorways
and shadows that change with the times, I walked
past a woman at whose glance I almost stopped cold,
almost to speak, to remind her of who I had been—
but walked on, not being certain it was she,
not knowing what I might find to say.
It wasn't quite the face I remembered, the years
being what they are, and I could have been wrong.

2

But that feeling of being stopped cold, stopped dead,
will not leave me, and I hark back
to the thing I remember her for, though God knows
how I could remind her of it now.
Well, one afternoon when I was fifteen
I sat in her class. She leaned on her desk,
facing us, the blackboard behind her arrayed
with geometrical figures—triangle, square,
pentagon, hexagon, et cetera. She pointed
and named them. "The five-sided figure," she said,
"is a polygon." So far so good, but then when she said,
"The six-sided one is a hexagon," I wanted things clear.
Three or more sides is *poly*, I knew, but five only
is *penta*, and said so; she denied it,
and I pressed the issue, I, with no grades
to speak of, a miserable average to stand on
with an Archimedean pole—no world to move,
either, just a fact to get straight, but she
would have none of it, saying at last, "Are you
contradicting me?"

3

A small thing to remember a teacher for. Since then,
I have thought about justice often enough
to have earned my uncertainty about what it is,
but one hard fact from that day has stayed with me:
If you're going to be a smartass, you have to be right,
and not just some of the time. "Are you
contradicting me?" she had said, and I stopped
breathing a moment, the burden of her words
pressing down through me hard and quick, the huge
weight of knowing I was right, and beaten. She
had me. "No, ma'am," I managed to say, wishing

I had the whole thing down on tape to play back
to the principal, wishing I were ten feet tall
and never mistaken, ever, about anything in this world,
wishing I were older, and long gone from there.

4

Now I am older, and long gone from there.
What sense in a grudge over something so small?
What use to forgive her for something
she wouldn't remember? Now students
face me as I stand at my desk, and the shoe
may yet find its way to the other foot,
if it hasn't already. I couldn't charge
thirty-five cents for all that I know
of geometry; what little I learned is gone now,
like a face looming up for a second out of years
that dissolve in the mind like a single summer.
Therefore,
if ever she almost stops me again,
I will walk on as I have done once already,
remembering how we failed each other,
knowing better than to blame anyone.

Virginia R. Terris

Born in 1917, Virginia Terris received a B.A. from the New Jersey College for Women in 1938, an M.A. from Adelphi University in 1964, and a Ph.D. from New York University in 1973. Among her books are an anthology, *The Many Worlds of Poetry* (1969), and two poetry collections, most recently *Tracking* (1976). She was a free-lance editor for twenty-five years at such New York publishing firms as Knopf and Random House and was a professor at Adelphi University from 1962 until 1983. Her poems have appeared in many magazines, including *Chelsea, New Letters, The American Poetry Review*, and *The New Yorker*. Terris has led many poetry workshops and has read her work both here and abroad. Her honors include residencies at Yaddo and other artist colonies and the Poetry Society of America's Gertrude B. Claytor Award.

Approaching Niagara

When I stepped from the bus
I heard the thunder from behind the trees
like the roaring from a throat that could not close.
I felt the ground trembling beneath me.
And there through the trees
I saw you walking
as you were before you imagined me
lovers on honeymoon touching one another.

Together you walked and I followed
toward the falls, the water gathering to leap.
You leaned against the railing glancing down
hand fondling hand. I watched
that huge current flowing beyond you
carrying in it trees it had uprooted
to shatter them on the rocks below
its mists rising
like the breath of an animal dying in winter.

Mary Tisera

Born in Williamsport, Pennsylvania in 1942, Mary Tisera received a
B.A. in urban studies from Chatham College and then attended the
Mercy Hospital School of Nursing. Her poems frequently appear in
such magazines as *West Branch, Kansas Quarterly, Poetry, The
Hudson Review, Tendril,* and *Milkweed Chronicle.* She lives in
Pennsylvania and currently works as a psychiatric nurse.

Three Voices in a Diner

Praise the lord, looks like snow again.
Any good soul spring for coffee?
Saving my bucks to build a new
box guitar. My aim to bring back
Rock and Roll, the pure music.
Sleep up the beach a ways. Where
the wind can't have at me. Pray
to Jesus and that wind whistles out
with the tide. My van's snug.
Got it stuffed with rags, the ceiling
wallpapered with news from
round the country. On days
when nothing happens, I lie back
and make out old news. Never the same
story grabs me. Know what went on
five years ago in Boise, that's
Idaho, the potato, and Houston

266

last month. Could've stayed there
but thought to catch spring beat
its drum along this coast. Besides,
we're flush with New York City
where they're hungry for talent.
Once I get my guitar in working
order, I'll head there. Here,
I got my van, my own tools,
good people like you two.
Got another cig I can borrow,
a match to spare? What brings you
all to Roy's? His old lady bakes
the pies herself. First rate. Uses
lard. None of that shortening shit.

Listen, young feller, you too old
to be knocking around, not settling
down to raise a peck of kids,
the wife, the house, the works.
Didn't hurt me none. The wife, she died.
I had to go somewheres. I figured
she always hankered to see the ocean.
What the hell: here I am.
Rooming house on the boardwalk, facing out.
The sun comes up bigger and redder
than back in Iowa. Could be
the water that makes the sun fan out.
I do just fine. Got my hotplate.
The landlady looks the other way.
And when her son's on the road
she invites me down.
Her corn fritters top drawer.
She's wise to my nipping too.
Didn't stop her from trotting
out the whiskey Christmas Eve.
If I was you I'd kick back home
while time's on your side. Now me,

I'm home as I'm ever going to get.
The undertaker can toss my bones
out to sea. Won't bother me a whip.
But you, you got your whole life,
box guitar or not. Rock and Roll
ain't the beginning, end of it.
If you clean yourself up
some girl will sure to turn
an ankle your way. 'Til the day she died
my Mabel had the ankles of a girl.
Can't beat that. Hey, Lady,
cat got your tongue? New to town?

Don't I wish. Just passing through. Here
we honeymooned seven years ago.
Some kind of joke, that, he choosing
our love nest to inform me
he's leaving next week. Right
this minute he's calling her
with the good news, or maybe flopped
in the twin bed mooning. Last time
we went King Size all the way.
Guess everything happens to plan.
Why else end where we began?
That first go round, summer,
we made love on the beach. This visit,
winter. And get this: he can't feature
being unfaithful to Carol. That's
her name. I had a cousin Carol.
Just think. Carol's been on call
all these years for her name
to land on my lips. Only
she couldn't know what she was
waiting for. Such innocents,
the lot of us—events in line,
itching to fall from some cosmic

conveyor belt. Hell, whatever
we do, wherever we go, life
overtakes us soon enough.
All this talk isn't worth the air
it's scribbled on. Hey guys,
anyone for pie? Come on,
I'm treating. Suppose this gesture
made to order, and if I hike
into the sea on a full stomach,
that too will be ordained.
Make mine apple, two scoops
vanilla on the side.

John Updike

Born in 1932, John Updike is a prolific fiction writer and poet. He was educated at Harvard University, where he contributed to *The Harvard Lampoon*, and graduated with top honors in 1954. Updike spent a year at the Ruskin School of Fine Arts in Oxford, England, and joined the staff of *The New Yorker* when he returned to the United States in 1955. He remained at the magazine for two years before beginning a career as a freelance writer. *Facing Nature* (Knopf: 1985) is his latest poetry collection. His honors include the Rosenthal Award in 1959 and the National Book Award in 1962.

Ode to Rot

Der gut Herr Gott
said, "Let there be rot,"
and hence bacteria and fungi sprang
into existence to dissolve the knot
of carbohydrates photosynthesis
achieves in plants, in living plants.
Forget the parasitic smuts,
the rusts, the scabs, the blights, the wilts, the spots,
the mildews and aspergillosis—
the fungi gone amok,
attacking living tissue,
another instance, did Nature need another,
of predatory heartlessness.
Pure rot

is not
but benign; without it, how
would the forest digest its fallen timber,
the woodchuck corpse
vanish to leave behind a poem?
Dead matter else would hold the elements in thrall—
nitrogen, phosphorus, gallium
forever locked into the slot
where once they chemically triggered
the lion's eye, the lily's relaxing leaf.

All sparks dispersed
to that bad memory wherein the dream of life
fails of recall, let rot
proclaim its revolution:
the microscopic hyphae sink
their fangs of enzyme into the rosy peach
and turn its blush a yielding brown,
a mud of melting glucose:
once-staunch committees of chemicals now vote
to join the invading union,
the former monarch and constitution routed
by the riot of rhizoids,
the thalloid consensus.

The world, reshuffled, rolls to renewed fullness;
the oranges forgot
in the refrigerator ''produce'' drawer
turn green and oblate
and altogether other than edible,
yet loom as planets of bliss to the ants at the dump.
The banana peel tossed from the Volvo
blackens and rises as roadside chicory.
Bodies loathsome with their maggotry of ghosts resolve
to earth and air,
their fire spent, and water there

as a minister must be, to pronounce the words.
All process is reprocessing;
give thanks for gradual ceaseless rot
gnawing gross Creation fine while we sleep,
the lightning-forged organic conspiracy's
merciful counterplot.

Constance Urdang

Born in New York City, Constance Urdang was educated at the Fieldston School, Smith College, and the University of Iowa Writers' Workshop. She has published one novel and four poetry collections, the latest being *Only the World* (Pitt Poetry Series). Coffee House Press recently released her novella *Lucha*. Urdang has received a National Endowment for the Arts Fellowship, a Carleton Centennial Award for Prose, and the 1981 Delmore Schwartz Memorial Poetry Award. She currently lives in St. Louis.

Mornings in Mexico

The sun behind a cloud,
The moon behind a tree;
On the speckled pavement
A lizard scurries without sound
And waits, with inexhaustible patience.

Here is a spray of butterflies,
A trembling mosaic of wings:
Take it, take it. Nearby,
Invisible as the air, a bird is singing.

This is no time for brooding over old wrongs;
Sighs, sighs—what a wearisome litany.
See where the plain is crisscrossed with goat-tracks

Weaving in and out of the clouds' shadows
All the way to the twilight-colored mountains.

The Old Ladies of Amsterdam

Indomitable, in black stockings, the old ladies of
        Amsterdam
Are pedalling their bicycles on the way to market.
Returning, with a chicken and some radishes,
How neatly they thread through the traffic,
Skilfully weaving in and out,
Dark figures in a sunlit tapestry.

Here are the canals of Amsterdam:
Green, sluggish, and redolent of gasoline.
It is raining on the canals. In January
They freeze. From across the Atlantic I see
The old ladies of Amsterdam balancing on silver skates,
Their black skirts whipping around their ankles.

I think I am with them, feeling a punishing wind
Bruise the afternoon on a deserted block
That had not been imagined when Amsterdam was old.
Behind an apartment window
An old lady pours pale tea from a Delft pot
In the honey-colored light of Vermeer.

Diane Wakoski

Diane Wakoski was born in Whittier, California in 1937, and received a B.A. from the University of California at Berkeley. After moving to New York City she worked as a book clerk and English teacher. In 1962 her first book of verse, *Coins and Coffins*, was published. She produced one of her most important works, *The George Washington Poems*, in 1967. Her latest book is *The Collected Greed Parts 1–13* (1984). Wakoski's many honors include the Robert Frost Fellowship, which enabled her to produce *Discrepancies and Apparitions* (1966), and grants from the Guggenheim Foundation and the National Endowment for the Arts.

On Saturn, After M
for Wallace Stevens at Key West

no sound
replaces an
idea, but the sound of your voice has become
a thought.
It comes back to me
as I sit on this morning terrace over the Pacific Ocean.
Wherever I am
          The Pacific Ocean
behind my eyes/
when I look at the streets of Cluj,
the mountains of Transylvania,
the voices speaking a language no more foreign

275

than the one in which
you said

goodbye

I always know
where I am.

Anne Waldman

Born in 1945 in Greenwich Village, New York City, Anne Waldman received a B.A. from Bennington College, where she studied with Howard Nemerov. She has edited two magazines, *Angel Hair* (which she co-founded with Lewis Warsh) and *The World*, as well as four anthologies. In addition, she has published over twenty poetry collections of her own. From 1968 until 1978 she directed the Poetry Project at St. Mark's Church-in-the-Bowery. In 1974 she and Allen Ginsberg founded the Jack Kerouac School of Disembodied Poetics at the Naropa Institute in Boulder, Colorado, where Waldman co-directs the recently accredited poetics program. She has been recorded as part of John Giorno's Dial-a-Poem Poets LP Series, and she performs her work internationally.

Walk Around Time

Girl bouncing red ball corner Sullivan & Spring Streets 1953
makes Spanish stucco so vivid so much paint everywhere Senior
    High
"I've always loved things like that"
Car up in the air, Grand Prix next?
Young men fingering tires & talking shop
"You have no instruction to use that Ed Sanders"
on by the wood shop and 3-ton truck
Yellow bleachers behind a green parka & endless cars with
students in motion
Government 6614 Nebraska "That's the coach's. I'll

introduce you as Oscar Robertson's buddy"
M's story "Monroe Wheeler At The Pumps" to mind
Smell of hot body shop, heh Cinderella!
Applied Math, Consumer Math & Algebra 1–2
taught by Miss Harms, Miss Carmen, Nelson Rockefeller
and Dave Van Ronk   Pink & yellow splotches
meet a corner above mounds of dirty ice
just like we have in New York City
now if I were a groundhog. . . . . . . I ain't
"Make gin outta those berries" Jack Collom says
pointing to juniper, hot house & mescal
from those cactus? geraniums in milk and remember
San Francisco's speckled leaves
Juniper like a flattop
cameos, Calculus Recourse, "Have to start kicking amen, man!"
a box springs & a faggot of wood for Magnolia Road
Christmas, Reed's poem with a "mum" in it
It is spring but
NO BEVERAGES IN THE GYM flagrant purple queer teeshirts
& a man speaking karate with an Asian accent
Video camera, kid waving scissors, containerized service
light through carnelian curtains in long ago empty room
light shifting slowly across wood
no one there the lone & level desks
sands of Nebraska raising arms to stretch

Robert Penn Warren

Robert Penn Warren was born in Guthrie, Kentucky in 1905, and was educated at Vanderbilt University. He originally intended to study science, but he was so taken with freshman English that he decided to study literature. As a student he met poet Allen Tate, who introduced him to the Fugitives, a poetry and philosophy society led by John Crowe Ransom. Warren furthered his studies at Yale University and at Oxford, on a Rhodes Scholarship. He taught at various colleges across the country before joining the Yale faculty in 1950. Warren is a noted novelist, poet, and critic. His novel, *All the King's Men* (1946), won a Pulitzer Prize, as did his poetry collection, *Promises* (1958). Warren also published an influential textbook, *Understanding Poetry*. *New and Selected Poems 1923–1985* is his latest book.

Question at Cliff-Thrust

From the outthrust ledge of sea-cliff you
Survey, downward, the lazy tangle and untangle of
Foam fringe, not on sand, but sucking through
Age-rotten pumice and lava like old fruitcake lost in an angle of
A kitchen closet, the fruit long since nibbled away
By mouse-tooth. This is a day
Of merciless sun, no wind, and
Of distance, slick as oil, sliding infinitely away
To no far smudge of land.
You stare down at your cove beneath.

No blackness of rock shows,
Only the gradual darkening green as depth grows.
In that depth how far would breath
Hold? Down through gull-torn air
You lean forward and stare
At the shelving green of hypnosis.

Who would guess
It would be as easy as this?

A pebble companions your white downward flash.
You do not hear what must be its tiny splash
As, bladelike, your fingertips
Into the green surface slash
And your body, frictionless, slips
Into a green atmosphere,
Where you can hear
Only the nothingness of sound, and see
Only the one great green and unforgiving eye of depth that
        steadily
Absorbs your being in its intensity.
You take the downward strokes, some two or three.
Suddenly your lungs, aflame, burn.
But there is the beckoning downwardness
That you must fight before you turn, and in the turn

Begin the long climb toward lighter green, and light,
Until you lie in lassitude and strengthlessness
On the green bulge of ocean under the sight
Of one gull that screams from east to west and is

Demanding what?

Michael Waters

Born in 1949, Michael Waters received a B.A. and an M.A. from the State University of New York at Brockport, an M.F.A. from the University of Iowa, and a Ph.D. from Ohio University. His first book, *Fish Light* (Ithaca House: 1975), was followed by *Not Just Any Death* (BOA Editions: 1979). *Anniversary of the Air* (Carnegie-Mellon: 1985) is his latest collection. Waters presently teaches at Salisbury State College. His honors include a fellowship from the National Endowment for the Arts.

A Romance

The couple arguing on Tenth Street—
"You've ruined it, Jenny," he shouts,
"you've ruined the Fourth of July!"—
halts my favorite waste of time:

reading titles on dust-jackets
lining the top shelves of bookcases
glimpsed through windows at night.
Jenny looks more than familiar—

once seen with some degree of intimacy.
Does anyone here recognize her?—
not the vendor on his corner
staining scoops of shaved ice—

cherry, lemon, grape—with patriotic
fervor, not the doberman
straining the leash to avoid them.
His voice carries to the upper stories.

Now I remember where I've seen her:
the inside cover of *The New Yorker*
modeling a Bali bra
in the lobby of some swank hotel.

Jenny rushes now through leaf-shadow
toward the clamor of Washington Square,
while the guy spits on the sidewalk,
then fixes me with his stare.

I return to the rows of books
luminous as a fireworks display:
THE AGE OF INNOCENCE, PORTRAIT OF A LADY,
LYRICS by Edna St. Vincent Millay.

Paul Zweig

Born in Brooklyn, New York in 1935, Paul Zweig received a B.A.
and an M.A. from Columbia University and a Ph.D. in comparative
literature from the Sorbonne. He was a literary critic, philosopher,
biographer, and a professor of comparative literature at Queens
College. *The Dark Side of the Earth* and *Against Emptiness* are his
first two poetry collections. His last book, *Eternity's Woods* (1985),
was published posthumously and is highly acclaimed by such poets
as David Ignatow and Charles Simic. Zweig lived in New York City
and Dordogne, France; he died in Paris at the age of forty-nine.

Snow

Love is all we could manage,
Its particles floating from the hard rim of the air.
Our tracks were clear in the fresh chance
Heaven threw behind us. The pain
Went on searching behind your face,
The snow went on falling.

Once your voice worked so gently into my brain,
It took root in the mind-dark
And branched forth again, singing.

Character may be a failure of love;
This morning, I want to love you,
And the birch trunks invisible on snow,

Your hand pushed warmly into my pocket;
I want to love the darkening blue at the
    sky's edge,
Our thoughts fumbling to hold on;
I want to love our breath-smoke warming
The air, then vanishing
In the frozen February day.

INDEX

Poet names are in bold; poem titles are in italics; poem first lines are in quotations.

ACKNOWLEDGMENTS

Permission to reprint copyrighted poems is gratefully acknowledged to the following:

ATHENEUM PUBLISHERS, INC., for "Grass" and "Topics" from *Late Settings* by James Merrill. Copyright © 1985 by James Merrill. "King Midas" from *A Winter Come, A Summer Gone* (1960) in *New Selected Poems* by Howard Moss. Copyright © 1985 by Howard Moss. "Sweet Will" from *Sweet Will* by Philip Levine. Copyright © 1985 by Philip Levine.

THE ATLANTIC MONTHLY PRESS, for "The Wellfleet Whale" from *Next to Last Things* by Stanley Kunitz. Copyright © 1985 by Stanley Kunitz.

JANE AUGUSTINE, for "For Meg." Copyright © by Jane Augustine. This poem first appeared in *Staple Diet*.

TINA BARR, for "Public Garden above the Rhone." Copyright © by Tina Barr (a.k.a. Elizabeth Barr). This poem first appeared in *Ploughshares*.

BEACH AND COMPANY, PUBLISHERS/CHERRY VALLEY EDITIONS, for "All the Women Poets I Like Didn't Have Their Fathers" from *Kiss the Skin Off* by Lyn Lifshin. Copyright © 1985 by Lyn Lifshin.

BEACON PRESS, for "Personal Pronoun I" and "It" from *Heredities* by Patricia Storace. Copyright © 1987 by Patricia Storace.

BLACK SPARROW PRESS, for "The Sickness" from *War All the Time: Poems 1981–1984* by Charles Bukowski. Copyright © 1984 by Charles Bukowski.

GEORGE BRAZILLER, INC., for "Watch Repair" from *Return to a Place Lit by a Glass of Milk* by Charles Simic. Copyright © 1974 by Charles Simic. "Happy End" from *Charon's Cosmology* by Charles Simic. Copyright © 1977 by Charles Simic.

DONALD BRITTON, for "In the Empire of the Air." Copyright © by Donald Britton. This poem first appeared in *The Paris Review*.

CARNEGIE-MELLON UNIVERSITY PRESS, for "A Romance" from *Anniversary of the Air* by Michael Waters. Copyright © 1985 by Michael Waters.

SUZANNE CLEARY, for "The Heart As Dog." Copyright © by Suzanne Cleary. This poem first appeared in *The Georgia Review*.

COFFEE HOUSE PRESS, for "Song Book" from *Margaret and Dusty* by Alice Notley. Copyright © 1985 by Alice Notley.

MARC COHEN, for "Blithe Cabbage." Copyright 1984 by Washington and Lee University. Copyright © by Marc Cohen. This poem first appeared in Shenandoah: The Washington and Lee University Review. Reprinted with the permission of the Editor and the author.

COPPER CANYON PRESS, for "Now We Must Wake the Sleepers and Prepare for the Night Journey," section 3 of part IV of *Letter to an Imaginary Friend* by Thomas McGrath. Copyright © 1985 by Thomas McGrath.

LYDIA DAVIS, for "The Dog Man." Copyright © by Lydia Davis. This poem first appeared in *The Paris Review*.

DAVID DENNY, for "Holden Caulfield at the Carwash." Copyright © by David Denny. This poem first appeared in the *Beloit Poetry Journal*.

TOI DERRICOTTE, for "Saturday Night." Copyright © by Toi Derricotte. This poem first appeared in *Pequod*.

TOM DISCH, for "The Size of the World." Copyright © by Tom Disch. This poem first appeared in the *Times Literary Supplement*.

DOUBLEDAY & COMPANY, INC., for, "A Third Body" from *Loving a Woman in Two Worlds* by Robert Bly. Copyright © 1985 by Robert Bly.

THE ECCO PRESS, for "Summer" and "5.Night Song" (from the poem "Marathon") from *The Triumph of Achilles* by Louise Glück. Copyright © 1985 by Louise Glück.

FARRAR, STRAUS & GIROUX, INC., for "What She Knew" from *Break It Down* by Lydia Davis. Copyright © 1976, 1981,

HOUGHTON MIFFLIN COMPANY, for "The Road Between Here and There" from *The Past* by Galway Kinnell. Copyright © 1985 by Galway Kinnell. "Sentimental Dangers" from *Saints and Strangers* by Andrew Hudgins. Copyright © 1985 by Andrew Hudgins.

FANNY HOWE, for "Franklin Park." Copyright © Fanny Howe. This poem first appeared in *Ironwood*.

THE HUDSON REVIEW, Vol. XXXVIII, No. 1 (Spring 1985), for "The Idea of a Town" by Richmond Lattimore. Copyright © by Richmond Lattimore.

DAVID IGNATOW, for "In Memoriam: For Sam." Copyright © by David Ignatow. This poem first appeared in *New Letters*.

ITHACA HOUSE, for "A Name" and "Sotto Voce" from *New Faces of 1952* by Maxine Chernoff. Copyright 1985 by Maxine Chernoff.

LAWRENCE JOSEPH, for "Any and All." Copyright © 1985 by The Modern Poetry Association. This poem first appeared in *Poetry*. Reprinted by permission of the Editor of *Poetry* and the author.

ALFRED A. KNOPF, INC., for "Ode to Rot" from *Facing Nature* by John Updike. Copyright © 1985 by John Updike. "Time" from *What the Light Was Like* by Amy Clampitt. Copyright © 1985 by Amy Clampitt. "Nothing More Will Happen" from *My Mother's Body* by Marge Piercy. Copyright © 1985 by Marge Piercy. "On Reading a Writer's Letters" and "Refrain" from *Henry Purcell in Japan* by Mary Jo Salter. Copyright © 1984 by Mary Jo Salter.

KENNETH KOCH, for "The Circus (I remember when I wrote 'The Circus')" from *Selected Poems 1950–1982* by Kenneth Koch. Copyright © 1975 by Kenneth Koch.

EDGAR KOERNER, for "Grandfather Ernst at Ebbets Field." Copyright © by Edgar Koerner. This poem first appeared in the *Manhattan Poetry Review*.

THE KULCHUR FOUNDATION, for "Walk Around Time" from *Invention* by Anne Waldman. Copyright © 1985 by Anne Waldman and Susan Hall.

JAMES LAUGHLIN, for "The Deconstructed Man" from *Se-*

Blond Okie" from *Black Hair* by Gary Soto. Copyright © 1985 by Gary Soto.

THE UNIVERSITY OF WISCONSIN PRESS, for "#3, Behind Chatham's Supermarket" from *Places/Everyone* by Jim Daniels. Copyright © 1985 by The Board of Regents of the University of Wisconsin System.

CONSTANCE URDANG, for "Mornings in Mexico" and "The Old Ladies of Amsterdam." Copyright © by Constance Urdang. These poems first appeared in *New Letters*.

VIKING PENGUIN INC., for "Lineage" from *A Short History of the Island of Butterflies* by Nicholas Christopher. Copyright © 1983 by Nicholas Christopher. "I Don't Know Her" from *Who Shall Know Them?* by Faye Kicknosway. Copyright © 1980 by Faye Kicknosway. "The Face in the Ceiling" from *Cemetery Nights* by Stephen Dobyns. Copyright © 1985 by Stephen Dobyns. "Oleum Misericordiae" from *Self-Portrait in a Convex Mirror* by John Ashbery. Copyright © 1975 by John Ashbery. "Getting Through" from *The Long Approach* by Maxine Kumin. Copyright © 1982, 1983, 1984, 1985 by Maxine Kumin. "I'm Not Complaining" from *Deep Within the Ravine* by Philip Schultz. Copyright © 1982 by Philip Schultz.

DIANE WAKOSKI, for "On Saturn, After M." Copyright © by Diane Wakoski. This poem first appeared in the *Manhattan Poetry Review*.

WESLEYAN UNIVERSITY PRESS, for "Snow" from *Eternity's Woods* by Paul Zweig. Copyright © 1985 by Ruthellyn Weiner, Executrix of the Estate of Paul Zweig.

WEST HILLS REVIEW, for "Mother's Day" by Susan Astor. Copyright © by Susan Astor. This poem first appeared in *West Hills Review*, volume 5, 1985.

YALE UNIVERSITY PRESS, for "Vines" from *Navigable Waterways* by Pamela Alexander. Copyright © 1985 by Yale University.